The

Perfect

Government

DEDICATION

This book is dedicated to all people who ever been involved in a political discussion and frustrated. To those who have ever heard a political speech and thought this guy is such a liar. To those who have questioned any of the seemingly irrational unfair or bizarre laws rules or things governments do. This book is for all the people who want to understand how the world works. All the seemingly irrational behavior and hypocritical behavior that seems to make no sense will now make perfect sense. This book is dedicated to all the former sheep who have come to realize that the shepherd does not have the best interest of his sheep as his foremost thought.

ACKNOWLEDGEMENTS

I would like to acknowledge all the talented intelligent, strong and steadfast people who have seen through the illusion the camouflage of the deceptive predators. I acknowledge All the people who have swum against the stream of popular opinion and peer pressure. I would like to acknowledge all the people who have made sacrifices to seek the truth and who stand courageously for the truth. When I was, younger I thought, I was alone in the way I thought but in the world of the Internet I now realize there are many others who have seen through the illusion of political deception. They realize a farmer doesn't love his cattle, a tapeworm does not love his host and the shepherd does not really have the best interest of his sheep in his heart.

PREFACE

It is with great relief that I write this book it is the culmination of many years of frustration and analysis. It is my hope that this book will clear up many people's confusion. Basically, this book explains everything. Why things are the way they are and why the world is the way it is. It is my hope that after reading this book you will sigh with relief and take comfort in seeing that everything fits together in a very logical way and makes perfect sense.

CONTENTS and INDEX

Chapter 1
The World Seems Crazy.

The world seems crazy.
The world is messed up.
It just doesn't make any sense.
It could be so much better. Citizens of America can't get healthcare yet the Congress gets free healthcare for life. Social Security is not enough for people to live on yet all our politicians get free benefits when they retire for life, yet people who vote for them don't thinks this is fair. Most Americans think there should be term limits to Congress but we don't have term limits. Congress has a 10% approval rating yet is one of the most secure jobs a person can get. Once someone gets into Congress they can almost never be removed. The political boundaries are gerrymandered so badly that no one new can ever get in power and change anything. Study after study has shown that politicians in general don't fulfill the will of the people. Yet the people have the right to vote and remove politicians but this never happens. Everyone in Congress becomes a millionaire but the job only pays $200,000 a year how is this possible? Doesn't simple math tell you that if you have 20 times as much money as you legally earn you must be getting it somewhere else?

The laws are also set up in a very crazy way. No one can understand them. If the robber comes into my house and steals my TV and my computer and slips on my floor injuring himself I might be sued. If I shoot the robber I might go to jail for 10 years or life. But if the robber shoots me he might go to jail for 5 years or not at all. The robber might plea-bargain down to a lesser charge. The laws are set up to help the few yet voting is done by the masses how is that possible? Why is the world the way it is? Nothing seems to make sense. Democratically elected governments are set up to help the few and powerful yet everybody gets a vote. How do these governments—elected by the majority-- victimize most the people? Criminals get coddled by the system yet hard-working, honest, productive people get penalized by the system. The list goes on. It can be seen in every level of life, from huge federal government down to the smallest little school board. Why are leaders of companies allowed to destroy the organization for their own personal profit and walk away with no consequences. The workers in these companies lose everything but the leaders of these companies lose nothing. Shouldn't the people who caused the problem lose instead of the people who didn't cause the problem? Why can a company dump millions of gallons of oil in the ocean and just pay a small fine, which doesn't hurt the leaders of the company at all, but if I dump a gallon of oil and in the ocean, I go to jail. Making a company pay a fine only hurts the stock holders who might be regular working people who have their retirement invested in the company and the government gets the money while the common people get nothing. How's come some people can owe the IRS hundreds of thousands of dollars for years and years and not go to jail but if I don't pay my taxes I will be punished that same year?

How do fools and unqualified people get good jobs? Why are so many stupid, inferior people put in charge of smarter, superior people? Why are school boards ineffective? Why is public education such a mess? Why are there so many crazy laws? Why is the tax code such a confusing mess? Shouldn't the tax code be so simple it's understood by everyone. Why don't people vote in people to help make the tax code simple and fair why is it unfair? Why are there so many unfair tax loopholes? Don't people want better government, better schools, better laws, a better society? Why do people treat each other so poorly? Why are cars only made to last a short time? Why do fashions keep changing? How does everything break right after the warranty goes out? Why do nice guys finish last? Why do people keep doing things that don't work? Why are so many politicians crooked? Why do lamb chops in a Midwest grocery store come from New Zealand; while the sheep farmer in the Midwest is going broke and can't sell his sheep? Is there something that makes shipping them across the world packed in ice cheaper than those grown down the road? Why do people keep voting the way they do? If everyone thinks things could and should be better, why aren't they? Why can't communism work? Why can't Socialism work? Why doesn't capitalism work?

I live in Hawaii but a computer made in japan can be shipped from Japan past Hawaii to California then taken off a boat loaded on a truck and hauled 2,000 miles to New York and then I can order that computer from a store in New York which will then ship it to me. Loading it on a truck in New York Then putting it on a plane then back tracking its original journey half way across the Pacific Ocean until it reaches Hawaii. I can buy this world traveling computer cheaper than I can buy a computer in Hawaii. This didn't make any sense.

If organic Farmers who want to grow organic they must spend a great deal of money and time filling out paperwork and being certified to prove that they don't spray pesticides and poisons on the crops yet mainstream farmers who spray pesticides and herbicides and fungicides on their crops don't have to fill out any paperwork to do that. So, it costs a great deal to not spray chemicals on your crops but if you choose not to spray the chemicals in your crops it costs you a great deal of time, effort and money this seems backwards and crazy shouldn't the farmers who used the chemicals have to fill out the paperwork and the farmers just doing it naturally not have to fill out anything?

People shake their heads and ask. Why are public schools a mess, why are politicians crooked, why doesn't anyone care about doing the right thing, why don't neighbors help each other anymore? People ask why" to hundreds of situations and questions. I was perplexed, and mystified, by this world that just does not seem right. Our world is not as good as it could be. It's not as good as it should be. It's a world that just didn't make sense. It just didn't add up.

All the questions can all be answered by the science of gaming theory and profit motive "why don't children have respect nowadays?" Well respect is not profitable for children to have now days and just as importantly disrespect is not unprofitable. It is that simple. These questions are answered by a proper understanding of simple economics and gaming theory and an understanding of how the rules of the game that have been set up by the government determines how people will play the game of life. You can now know why the world is messed up and take comfort in the fact that it all now makes perfect sense.

CHAPTER 2
There is a reason for everything (The world is not crazy) (There is a logical reason for everything)

The world is not crazy there is a reason for everything. Even if we don't understand the reason. This chapter will explain why although it seems society is directed in several contradictory, confusing directions it really is not. It may seem impossible but soon everything in the world, every crazy messed up thing will now make perfect sense. It will be quite a relief to understand how the world works and why our government is the way it is. Nothing is confusing, if you look at government logically, it all makes sense. If you can understand gaming theory and profit motive everything will be explained. Just because a caveman did not understand why wood burned and released heat he did not understand the actual chemical processes. Did not mean there was no logical reason for that. It was not messed up, or strange or magic. It was just beyond his knowledge at that time, beyond his present understanding. Just because many people today don't understand why things are the way they are, doesn't mean there's not a logical reason for them. It is the purpose of this book to show people the logic behind every day human interactions.

First, we must be able to look behind this curtain, and understand the real mechanism behind government programs. We must understand that anything advertised to help reduce problems is not there to reduce the problem. Things that increase the problem cannot reduce the problem. Rewarding lazy, irresponsible, victimized, people only makes the situation worse because now it is profitable to be lazy, irresponsible, and a victim. Another reason why it can never work is because, any program in which it is possible to cheat will be cheated. If cheating is a benefit people will cheat. Any system set up can be taken advantage of if the system does not have safeguards already put in place to stop cheating which almost no government program does. Any situation set up that has a possibility to be taken advantage of will be taken advantage of. This is true whether you are talking about mice, birds, bees, weeds, chimps, dolphins or humans. A squirrel will eat out of a bird feeder any chance he gets. He does not avoid the birdfeeder because it's for birds and not for squirrels. A crack whore will buy drugs with food stamps she does not differentiate between government aid for food or government aid for drugs any more than a squirrel differentiates between food for squirrels or food for birds. Another reason that government programs don't work is because individuals have a single mind and purpose and can react faster than a huge government body. A huge committee cannot respond like a single mind. In government is the hugest committee.

Government social policies that encourage irresponsible behavior if they suddenly make these behaviors profitable. The behaviors they supposedly want to reduce are now rewarded. It is now beneficial to be a victim. People will do what benefits them. Every action is selfish and people will only do what benefits them. For example, in strict Muslim countries it is very unprofitable to steal. You could get your arm cut off or be killed. But in some other countries it is very profitable to steal. Your risk of getting caught is low, and even if you are caught the punishment may be minor so it is worth the risk. In some cases, it is certainly less than the risk of being a legitimate business man. The man who takes his life savings and

invests it into a business with a 75% chance of failure takes a great risk. Most starting small businesses fail those are just the realistic odds. In this case, it is more profitable to steal than work. To invest in a legal business requires more work and risk than stealing. But this is because of the environment, the system we live under. This is so pervasive in American society that the examples are numerous and at every level. Free breakfast at schools means it is now profitable to not feed your children breakfast because the government will do it for you. The government will give you money if you have children you can't afford and the more children you have that you can't afford the more money, government will give you. There are 75 IQ teenage girls with absolutely no talent who can make more money receiving government payments for having children out of wedlock than any legitimate job they could hold. If you don't have any skills this might be your most profitable course of action. Why would you not take your most profitable course of action. All the things that seem illogical or insane are very logical and sane, very reasonable if you do three things:
1. Apply gaming theory to the situation.
2. Ask what is the profit or who actually profits.
3. Ask what are they selling.
There is a harsh old saying that sums up human interactions.
"Remember your mother might love you
but everyone else is selling something."
And this is only because your mother has so much invested in you that her best, most selfish, most logical course of action is to help you out a great deal. Anything that is profitable will be done. If it is profitable or beneficial to cheat then cheating will be successful. If it is beneficial for businessmen to cheat

then successful business men will cheat. Unsuccessful businessmen will not cheat and so go out of business and they will cease to exist. Unsuccessful businessmen will go out of business leaving only cheaters in the business world. Is very logical to see why there are so many dishonest people. The non-cheaters cannot compete with the cheaters. It will be too great a handicap to overcome. The case is even more so in the political world. This is also why no 100% honest politicians can ever get into office. This is also why no government program has ever worked, ever can work, or ever will work. For any system to work, it must start out with a stable strategy and take into account gaming theory, and profit motive, and the law that there will never go and unexploited resource. It is the purpose of this book to very clearly and simply explain these principles.

Chapter 3
Gaming Theory

Gaming theory explains everything we see in life including the government and the natural world. All Murder stealing, lying, bullying, loyalty, sharing, greed, kindness, generosity, compassion, honesty, self-sacrifice, everything we consider positive and every trait we consider negative is explained by gaming theory. If you understand the context of any action you will see that every action is selfish. Even if the actions are considered selfless and appear selfless they are still selfish you just can't recognize it yet. The behavior of an organism determines if that organism is successful if it lives or dies if it's genes exist or disappear. Creatures behavior can seem complicated but one easy way to simplify the understanding of it is to use gaming theory. With the gaming matrix, we can see very easily which actions are going to win and which actions will lead to losing. In the gaming matrix, just like life the cost of each decision, of each choice, of each action has consequences measurable consequences. And with the gaming matrix we can run a million lifetimes in a minute and see what the result of a thousand years of government programs will lead to and do it very quickly.

Gaming theory explains all human behavior, in fact not just human behavior but the behavior of all life forms on the planet is explained by gaming theory. One simple example of gaming theory that everyone knows is called the prisoner's dilemma. In this example, the police question two men who they suspect may have committed a crime. There are four possible outcomes. If neither confesses to the crime and both stick to their story, both men will go free. The police do not have enough evidence or a strong enough case to convict them and send the men to jail. If one man betrays the other man and will make a confession, he takes a plea deal, he will get 2 years in jail but the other man will get 10 years in jail. And like-wise if during questioning one man does not confess and stays loyal, but his partner has betrayed him he will get 10 years while the betraying partner gets 2 years. This is where the dilemma comes into play. The best thing for both men to do is to stick to their original story and not confess—each man will go free. However, the police separate the men into two different rooms. Now, how can each man be sure the other hasn't sold him out? Criminals are not known to be all that morally upright—what if the partner betrayed him? If he does not betray his partner and his partner betrays him, he will get ten years. Can he risk it? Neither can be sure the other hasn't sold him out. He can't take that chance. The maximum good for both is to just keep silent. That would be the most profitable course of action. This will not be the case if neither has absolute faith in the other's loyalty. Police get many confessions using this principle. In fact, in real life most of the time the police get their confessions. The threat of more jail time without a confession, makes it profitable to betray your partner and Potentially expensive to remain loyal to your partner. As an interesting aside, I am told that the Hell's Angels motorcycle gang has never had a felony conviction. One reason might be because to betray another member of the Hell's Angels would be far more expensive than jail time. So, in that case the gang member is simply maximizing his profit, avoiding the stick and seeking the carrot. There are millions of interactions people have every day with everyone and everything, the IRS, with the neighbor, with their children, with their boss, etc. and the result of every single one of these interactions is predicted with 100% accuracy by gaming theory.

The power of gaming theory to predict real world outcomes in very impressive. One thing that is reviled by gaming theory is that if you want to remove all goodness out of a system, society, culture, company, business, or government all you have to do is simply remove the profit for being good and it will disappear. One example, of basic goodness is the love and sacrifice for family this is perfectly explained by science. This is called Kin Selection. The definition of reproductive success is to leave as many copies of your genes in the next generation as possible. Now, many short sighted, people think the best way to do that is by having children. A child is 50% of its mother and 50% of its father. If you have 2 children, both of them added together have equal value genetically as you do by yourself. Brothers and sisters also share 50% of their genes. Your mother and father also share 50% of your genes. From the cold economic viewpoint of reproductive success, in a gaming matrix if you could jump off a cliff and sacrifice yourself to save your mother, father, brother, sister, son, and daughter it is profitable. These 6 people each share 50% of your genes. Together they have 300% of your genetic material. If you lose 100% to save 300%, it is a bargain. A 200% profit! You only contain 100% of your genetic material.

This also works out in interesting ways for risk taking and sacrifice for family members things generally labeled as unselfish but that are really selfish and explained by gaming theory. If your brother is drowning and you jump in to save him, with a 40% chance of drowning and a 60% chance of saving him while staying alive, it is profitable for you to do so. If it is more dangerous, say a 90% chance of dying in trying to save him, it is no longer a bargain and becomes unprofitable. If a mother has two children hanging on to the north side of a cliff and one child hanging on the south side of the cliff and she only has time to throw a rope to one side her best, most profitable most selfish action is to throw it to the north side hopefully saving 2 of her 3 children.

With first cousins, the percentages are different. You only share 12.5% of the same genes with your cousin so it is not profitable to take as big a risk to save you cousin as it would be to save your brother. A risk of 50% death to save a brother is the breakeven point but to try and do a heroic rescue of a cousin with 50% risk of death is unprofitable i.e. a bad investment. If your cousin and your own child where both drowning and you were pure profit motive driven, you would save your own child first. Your nieces and nephews share 25% of your DNA so you should from a purely profit driven decision value your nephew twice as much as your cousin.

Once you understand gaming theory you can see that self-sacrifice, greed, generosity, kindness, and selfishness are all the same thing. All driven by strategy to win at gaming theory. It is pure selfishness and maximizing profit in the gaming matrix of life. We just give those actions different names. The examples of kin selection in nature are almost endless. In another well-known example: a prairie dog sees a hawk and barks an alarm. Now he has drawn the hawk's attention to himself. His risk of being killed by the hawk has slightly increased. A person might think that the best thing for him to do from a purely self-interest viewpoint is to watch the hawk kill one of his neighbors and be silent. Creationists used to use this as an example of facts which argue against Darwinian evolution. This would be true however there are many other things going on. For example, many of the prairie dogs in that town are related to him: brothers, sisters, cousins, second cousins, third cousins, fourth cousins, aunts, uncles, etc. who share his genes so saving them each times saves small parts of himself. Other facts to consider are that the better fed a hawk is the more likely he is to make his next kill which might be him next time. Also, the more food a hawk brings home the more young hawks the hawk can raise which means more hawk predators in the future. Another factor is the more fragmented and destroyed the prairie dog town is, the less likely it is to compete successfully against another prairie dog town. There are many unnoticed factors and consequences that relate to an interaction than are readily apparent. This situation seems very complicated and goes beyond the simple tic tat too box of only two choices of the classic prisoner's dilemma but if you were to take every single factor and assign it a proper value, making a box of many rows and columns it would all add up and show that every action in nature is 100% selfish. In fact, in nature we see exactly what we would predict based on the simple math and simple economics of gaming theory no mystery at all.

The more related a species is in a group, pack, flock, nest, etc., the more seemingly unselfish are their members. Bees ants and termites are Eusociality which is the scientific word meaning the highest level of organization of animal sociality. But how and why can this be. Well bees ants and other Eusocial insects develop from an unfertilized egg in this haplodiploid sex-determination system the relatedness between workers (diploid females) in a hive or nest is 75% This means the workers are significantly more closely related than in other sex determination systems where the relatedness of siblings is 50%. Now, this means that the whole beehive is even more closely related to each other than are full-blooded mammal brothers and so should according to gaming theory be even more cooperative, self-sacrificing and group oriented. As gaming theory predicts this is exactly what we see in nature. A bee will willingly sting an intruder to protect the hive, killing itself, but saving thousands of its 75% related siblings which according to gaming theory is a bargain. So, you see, it is profitable or beneficial for a bee to sacrifice itself to save its hive. Bees have established a society in which self-sacrifice and altruism are profitable for the individual. It is in everyone's own selfish best interest to not be selfish. Now this may seem to be an oxymoron it is in your own selfish best interest to not be selfish! Are bee's ants and termites the most unselfish, most altruistic most self-sacrificing creatures on the planet? no. They are simply like every other creature maximizing their profit in gaming theory and acting in the most selfish, self-serving, and profitable way they can. According to gaming theory a bee who dies protecting its hive is as selfish as an investment banker embezzling all the banks funds. It is acting in the most selfish way possible.

We will see that Eusocial insects are no more generous to the group than any other traitorous human. In bee, ant and termite colonies the males are born then they mate their sperm is stored in the queen and then they are killed. Why waste resources on unneeded males when all that is needed is their sperm? Now this seems rather selfish for such unselfish critters. Why not just let the males live, surely a single drone bee in a hive wouldn't drain that many resources, couldn't a bee hive just show a little kindness, a little bee welfare. The answer seems to be "no." According to gaming theory that would not work in the long run and according to what we see in nature that is true. Gaming theory exactly predicts what we see in nature. If there were a kind queen who did let some males live, it would be unprofitable. Those males would drain some resources away from the hive. Maybe the hive could afford to lose some resources. Out of a million bees a single extra male drone would not even be noticed, right? It seems that way, however in the real world we don't see this behavior so it must not work. It would be one millionth less efficient than a hive that killed it's no longer needed drones so would be outcompeted over a million generations. Mother nature is a much more ruthless, efficient, cold and calculating manager then any CEO of Wall Street could ever hope to be. For the same reason that you don't see generous male lions you will not see generous beehives. In the bee world a more selfish, more efficiently run hive with that 0.000,1 percent advantage would out compete the kind, nice gentle queen and her hive.

This trait must have cropped up a few times in the past hundred million years and even the haploid chromosomes of drones are inconsistent so this trait might still be in the experimental stage evolutionarily speaking but as far as I know it is completely dominated by the most efficient model just as we would predict using gaming theory.

Remember Mother nature is far more ruthless and efficient than account or being counter of any company. And this is the beauty and power of gaming theory especially when it can be played out a billion times in a computer simulation and not just a simple tic tac toe box with paper and pencil by hand. A .0001% advantage is tiny, Las Vegas has relatively huge about a 2% advantage. It takes people a long time to realize with their 48% chance of winning against Las Vegas with a 52% chance of winning that in the long run game after game, interaction after interaction Las Vegas will eventually win. If everybody went to Las Vegas and gambled for a long enough time everyone would lose. But if people only go 6 times in their life they may win 3 times and lose 3 times it's not that noticeable. So human beings don't get a full understanding of gaming theory physically playing the gambling games in Las Vegas only half a dozen times. But if we use computers and modeled those games in Las Vegas and ran the interactions hundreds of millions of times we would see that Las Vegas in the long run always wins. Which is exactly what Las Vegas does spreading out its games among hundreds of millions of people. In a similar case in nature over millions of years of evolution the termite and in bee colonies with a .0001% advantage have exterminated, outcompeted the other bee colonies who no longer show any of this less efficient, unstable, unprofitable behavior. The kind bee's hives have lost out to the more efficient, ruthless, bee hives just like a more efficient business will out compete a less efficient business barring of course government interference. And it seems to be one of the purposes of modern American government is to keep the less efficient, less stable, less unprofitable behaviors, actions, and habits from going extinct like they do in the natural world.

Now this is where the Communists, Socialists, globalists, liberals, social justice warriors, and all-round do-gooders mess everything up. We have always had a difference between the theoretical optimum, pie-in-the-sky, dream strategy; verses the realistic, real-life, stable strategy. Since gaming theory explains and describes everything we see in nature, every mother nursing a baby, every father

24

spanking the child, every father allowing a child to backtalk, every man getting married, every man decided not to get married, every woman getting married, every lion killing the previous male lion's cubs, what is really is best strategy to have for life. What is the most efficient and effective way to play the game. If you could take your entire life's decisions and interactions and weigh each decision perfectly, put them in a gaming matrix and play them out millions of times on a computer. You would know exactly the correct course of action to use in your life for the best results. This would be an amazingly helpful bit of information to have.

Well it just so happens we can do that. With the use of computers and a gaming theory matrix we can run billions of games, with billions of input values and find out exactly what is the best strategy for life. Anyone can set up a game matrix and how closely it matches real life depends on what numbers you assign it. In this book, I will explain the very simplest gaming matrix but I think it will illustrate how gaming theory works and why it is so powerful at predicting behavior. Imagine you have a tic-tac-toe box or a pair of cards. You have two options: cheat or help. You may place any value you want on actions in the game. For the sake of illustration let's make up a game. You get two cards one that says help and one that says cheat. So you can only play one of two cards. Help or Cheat as can your neighbor. You have only four possible outcomes. If your neighbor helps you and you cheat him, you get 10 points and he gets 0 points. If your neighbor helps you and you help him you each get 7 points. But if your neighbor plays the chief card and you play the cheat card, you each get 2 points. Remember if you help your neighbor and he cheats you, then you get 0 points. There are four possible payouts 10 or 7 or 2 or 0. Now what is the best strategy to accumulate the most points. You can't do better than 10 points every turn. That is the maximum possible number of points you could win. For that to happen your neighbor would have to help you every turn, while you never helped him. He would basically have to agree to be taken advantage of every single time. No one really does the "turn the other cheek thing" or the "if my enemy makes me carry his pack 1 mile I will carry it 2 miles" or the "I will forgive my neighbor 70 times 7 times". Those are obviously unstable strategies that would only lead to extinction for the animal, tribe, business, or government that tried it. Most neighbors will not loan you a shovel, then you not loan them anything. They pull you out of a ditch; let you borrow a cup of sugar or whatever indefinitely without some reciprocity on your part. If they continue to do this it would be most profitable for you to keep cheating them and you would get 10 points every turn, which is the maximum theoretical value. It is not a realistic value because no one would keep letting you cheat him or her every time. Now in this imaginary gaming matrix if you played this game with a single other person you might be able to eventually just agree to play cooperate, cooperate each time and get 7 points per turn. But as you added more people into the group people you did not know nor trust who had the ability to play the chief card at any given opportunity the game would become more complicated. And computer simulations can make the game incredibly complex. A computer can be programmed with a million different players each with a different strategy. Is there any strategy that tends to work in a very complicated game with millions of different players? What strategy tends to win over all the other strategies. When a computer simulation is run the computer can have everyone using a different strategy to win the game? There are an endless number of strategies on how to play the game and it gets more complex as you add players from 2 all the way to millions. With a computer playing the game, you could try anything From "turn the other cheek", "always help no matter what", and "forgive others wrongs" to the other extreme of "cheat everyone every chance you get" and try to get 10 points every time. Still more complicated strategies might include "cheating every third time" and "cheating at random so others can't find a pattern" or "cheat only when you think you can get away with it" or a limitless number of other ones. I once saw on some pie in the sky day time show the idea of lets just do a win win because that would get the most points and the audience claps. But this is so dishonest, offer that same audience a prize of $1 million for only the winner of this game and watch the audience of kind people change. Such a reality show would be interesting to watch. A scientist could sit down with a pencil and paper and draw a box and divide it into four squares and play this game out a hundred times and see what strategy wins most often. That would only be comparing two certain strategies against each other. Sometimes strategy 1 might beat strategy 2, and 2 might beat 3, but 3 might beat 1 so the paper work of comparing hundreds of different strategies over thousands of games would be enormous. Thanks to modern computer technology we can play a thousand different strategies over a million games all competing and see what wins. Then we could change the values a little and play them a million more times to see what wins. We could make cooperation more valuable or less valuable. This might model a society in which someone not cooperating would never have business or someone not cooperating is relatively anonymous. Or try making cheating and betrayal more profitable or less profitable. This might mimic a society which cuts the arms off the thief versus a government that lets the thief go with no punishment or very little or gives them 2nd and 3rd and 4th chances. Social scientists try to plug in a range of values that approximates real life in American society based on the laws of American Government. And see what happens, remember a computer and can play billions of rounds a second with this game which would simulate a society after many thousands of years. Gaming theory will accurately predict if and when a society will collapse. This ultimately and clearly predicts with great accuracy if that society will go extinct or not. So, what is the best way to behave? Well it depends on the environment and what the government rewards or punishes. However, what if there was no outside government controls what is the best strategy? It is interesting that one pattern tends to emerge as the winning strategy. It is called "nice tit for tat". Basically, the strategy is this. You start out nice, that is you always try to do good to your neighbor on your first encounter. Then you just follow your neighbors lead. Simply respond as your neighbor did. If your opponent helps you, then you help him, and continue to do this every time until he cheats you. If your neighbor cheats you then you cheat him back. But if he begins to help you again you do give him a 2nd chance and start to help him again. It doesn't even seem to be profitable to hold grudges. This game has been played where one player after cooperating for a long series and then they get cheated once uses the strategy of getting even and turning over the cheat card twice. Once after the neighbor cheated you and once even after the neighbor played cooperate. This

28

getting even and holding a grudge even for one turn doesn't seem to be the most profitable strategy. Could it be the real world is set up to reward those who forgive? Many variations on this have been tried. You could start out bad, until your opponent proved he was good. Or you can punish a bad neighbor with three betrayals for every one he gave you. You could start out nice, but never deal with anyone once they betrayed you. You can cheat every time or at random so no pattern can be established and on and on and on with no limit to the imagination. It seems that the simple almost intuitive nice guy "tit for tat" seems to be about the best you can do to maximize you profit in the game of life. It is about the best overall strategy. For the sake of simplicity let's say this strategy averages about 6 points a turn. After a million turns, you have 6,000,000 points. This is well shy of the highest possible 10,000,000 points and shy of the best theoretical, 7,000,000 points if everyone would just always cooperate and be good little communists. But it's about as good as you can get in the real world. And this is where the mistake the liberals make starts. They insist that a government can force a society to behave in such a way that everyone averages 7 points per turn for every interaction.

It is through the social engineers, communists, socialists, liberals, leftists, globalists, do-gooders, etc. trying to achieve the theoretical 7 points per turn that we have gotten into so many problems. This is why the world is messed up and our government messed it up. Can you imagine some big liberal socialist or communist saying we are going to make sure everyone gets 7 points per turn, every turn; we will redistribute the wealth? They will need to hire government officials to watch the game. This not only bleeds off part of the 7 theoretical possible points because now we must pay people to watch the game and the government by taking points from everyone to pay for itself to watch the game makes less points available for everyone else. But this is not even the worst problem. This concentration of power this bureaucracy gives power to some people over others. Instead of everyone being on an even playing field deciding for themselves which card they will turn over be it, cooperate or cheat and then suffering the consequences of their decision to play cooperate or cheat. We now have a giant anonymous government that can coerce people into playing one card or the other and never personally suffer the consequences of the card played. Some people can take bribes because they are in positions of power they would not have otherwise. It requires some people to watch others and even the watchers need to be watched so the watchers of the watchers, those people must be paid which bleeds off more of the set theoretical seven points possible. I find it amazing in discussing with liberals that any time a problem with government corruption is pointed out their solution is to always add another layer of government. Its idiotic to me to say to someone X caused a problem and the person to respond by saying see, we need more X.

Government is so big and powerful that it can ignore the peoples wishes and do whatever it wants, so the leftist's solution is to add another layer of Government? I am as frustrated at hearing this as a cancer patient who went to his doctor and heard the doctor say that to cure your cancer we will have to add more cancer to your body because the current cancer cells you have are not behaving. Government must get money to pay for the guards, spies, watchers, police etc. which bleeds even more resources from the theoretical 7 points which is about as close as a small family group or tribe or stable commune or group of pirates can get. The government now must establish something like a game tax. to pay for the game. Remember, everyone is in the game, even the guards it's like a giant pyramid scam that that no one can leave. It is like hiring the foxes to guard the chickens. It is now in the guard's best interest to have some cheating going on to justify their salary. They will now pass laws to prevent game players from defending themselves from cheaters, they will now house and feed cheats, pay for cheats medical care, charge a fee to administer the game. They may even pass laws making things that no one cares about a crime so they can create more crime. This could be like the laws against pot. Well over 50% of Americans don't agree with many laws but we have them anyway. But those laws support over 50% of judges, lawyers, police, prison, court ordered drug rehab, medical personal etc. and these people who are empowered by those rules, who would not have jobs without those laws are benefiting greatly from these laws, which most American citizens don't agree with don't want and if allowed to vote on their phones or could discuss it in a giant Internet forum would all agree to drop them. Because these laws exist it is now necessary to hire police to watch the game and make sure everyone plays fair but of course not everyone is caught. There's an old saying recognized by thinkers for the last 2000 years.

"(Laws are like spider webs, they capture the weak and vulnerable while the strong and mighty walk through them.)"

The police can't catch every cheater but more importantly, they don't want to. So they still make it profitable to cheat, you just must be more careful or become friends with the cops or bribe the cops with a percentage of your profit from cheating, or have a lawyer who is politically connected. With lawyers and courts and judges working the system, each caught cheater now gets 10 chances at cheating before punishment and he didn't get caught cheating the first time. He probably only gets caught cheating every 10th time he did it. Cheating is now profitable because the cheater, i.e. the criminal gets 10 points per turn before they are penalized for it; i.e. fines, arrest, or whatever. They hire a lawyer. Of course, you now need a judge. Before you realize it, the slippery slope has slid down so low everyone is averaging 4 points per turn in the game. Instead of the 6 everyone would earn just doing it as free enterprise. It is now even more far removed from the theoretical 7 points per turn that the idealists, socialists, Statetheists, communists, collectivists, dreamed of. Which is exactly what we see in real life. All of these communist countries have a much lower standard of living than the freer countries which is exactly what we expect with a minor understanding of gaming theory. Would you rather live in North Korea or South Korea? Communist China or Taiwan? That choice is a perfect real-world example of this.

Many of the controllers, the communists, the leftists, wring their hands and cry if we could just do communism or socialism or big government better everyone could get 7 points per turn and life would be so good. It would be the most good for the most people. We must raise taxes. Make government bigger. Expand control, because it obviously isn't big and controlling enough. Now this ignores two points of reality. 1 that people are selfish and will always grab and extra cookie when they can get away with it. Not every human is completely brain washed to the point of an insect in the hive collective of what can I do to help my fellow ants every second. And 2 every layer of watcher from the government who is put in place as a safe guard is an added expense or cost, basically a parasite to the free movement of goods and services. This is why so many artificial, man-made government programs don't work. They never solve the problems they were designed to fix. It is also why we so often see, in real life, also called reality, the example of a solution to a problem being worse than the problem. This is the reason all communist countries are also big human rights violators. It is simply the nature of the beast, a government big enough to give you everything is big enough to bully you. A government big enough to give you everything, is big enough to take everything from you. There is no way to make a government big enough to give you everything, and protect you from everything, watch everything and squish people's ability to be selfish and not make it big enough to be able to take everything from you. This is another one of the lapses of logic I hear from socialists. People are bad and evil and individuals have too much power and cause harm, so let's give lots of power to a small, anonymous collection of people who have absolutely no interest in your benefit and are invulnerable to any retaliation. In fact, these people who run the big government have no knowledge you even exist as an individual, your pain means nothing to them, in your suffering can affect them zero. Yet somehow, they should do everything for you and have your best interest at heart? That is arrogant in the most extreme.

A large government is simply a collection of

individuals and as can be seen by gaming theory those individuals will do what benefits them the most. To assume strangers, love and care for you out of the goodness of their heart or because your fate is important to them is arrogant beyond belief. No social problem that does not specifically hurt or pain the rich politician in charge will be solved by the rich anonymous politician unless it specifically benefits him. And like every selfish person in power or out of power it is the bribe or kickback that motivate his behavior. Remember according to gaming theory every person will simply do the action which benefits them the most personally.

The examples of this gaming matrix in government are endless. There is a social problem of too many babies being born to unwed teen-age mothers, who can't support their children or care for their children. These teenage and or unwed mothers don't provide basic care for their children, they don't read to them, they don't nurse them, they don't make sure they have adequate sleep etc. Basically, there is a problem in the United States of women who have babies but don't raise them well. So, to solve this problem the United States government gives money to unwed teenage mothers paying and rewarding her for every baby she produces, but only if the child has no father and the mother can't provide for the child. Every child a mother produces but cannot care for causes money to flow in from the government. However, every carefully, responsibly, planned child produced by a responsible mother and father will receive zero money from the government. Now anyone with a brain, some reasoning ability and an understanding of gaming theory can see what is going to happen. But the American government acts surprised or pretends to act surprised and complains about the increasing number of children born in poverty to mothers who don't raise them. It may seem that I am using humor known as sarcasm but really this is true. The American government really rewards women for having babies they are not capable of taking care of and punishes women who are having babies that they are capable taking care of. Money will not be given to a mother if a father is present working a job trying to support his child. The result of all this government help is obvious and predictable. All the responsible fathers have been driven out of the ghetto just as gaming theory would predict. Responsible fathers are not encouraged, promoted or helped by Americas government. Now it has become profitable to be a teen-age unwed mother and have a baby. In the present gaming situation with no job skills a woman can receive a check just for reproducing before she can take care of her children.

But if you are responsible and wait to reproduce until you can care for your children you receive no reward. Nothing is given for good behavior in fact you are punished. This is because money is taken from you in the form of taxes. This money could have benefited your children in any number of ways, more books, better food, vitamins, summer vacation, collage fund piano lessons etc. But this is not the way government has set up the game. Money is taken from the responsible mothers and given to the irresponsible mothers who can't or won't care for their children. Now the irresponsible mother has had her resources freed up to produce more children because she will get even more money from the government for producing another child she is unable to care for. Now you may think this is crazy, insane and totally lacks logic but if you sit back and look at the situation with gaming theory and profit motive in mind it makes perfect sense. As gaming theory would predict every group is simple playing the card doing the action which returns the most profit back to them. The welfare mom is doing what profits her the most. Which is having babies and being paid for it. The government agency welfare organization is doing what benefits it the most, that is increasing its client base just like any company would do i.e. increasing its numbers of customers and increasing its client base.

Is it really in the welfare systems own best interest to put itself out of business? Of course not. No system, organization, government program, commits suicide? Remember the government agency doesn't love welfare parents or kids. They love themselves and only work for themselves. The cost of administrating welfare is enormous, think of all the administrators involved in welfare they benefit from welfare. The government administrators benefit from welfare more than the welfare recipients does you must learn to follow the money and see who really benefits if you want to see how government really works. If every dime spent on welfare was used for education then every person on welfare could have been sent to Harvard. If every dime spent on welfare was given to the poor person they could have bought their own house and retired with a stock portfolio. The politician who votes for welfare is acting in his own self-interest the money he sends to welfare is someone else's money so it costs him nothing. He is selling compassion, he is getting votes, he is increasing his voter block. Welfare profits him because these people are now dependent on him. Millions of dollars handed out to welfare don't cost him a dime remember it's not his money, he is not giving away his money so he can afford to be generous with another people's money. This is like the Hollywood millionaire who lives in a gated community, with fences and armed guards and has 6 mansions in 6 different countries getting on TV and telling everyone else they are selfish for not sharing their wealth and they should open their houses and borders to foreigners who might take their jobs or destroy their neighborhood. They are doing what value them what profits them because in their lifestyle and their neighborhood they will never see any of the common people. It costs them nothing to make this statement and gains them lots of free publicity and goodwill. According to gaming theory they are simply doing what profits them the most This is another point somehow the idea that someone gives away tax money or giving away another person's property is kind and generous seems to permeate modern politics. But the politician who fights to save the taxpayer money and not give away someone else's money but let that person keep their own money is painted as evil and selfish. In reality, the most selfish thing a politician can do is spend other people's money. The most generous thing a politician can do is not spend other people's money. Because no politician is spending his own money. It is amazing to me how many people get this simple fact backwards.

Of course, anyone reading this book would now understand that this is part of the camouflage of government. The leopard uses camouflage to sneak up on a gazelle it is a deception and all war is deception and all politics is deception. If someone can pretend to be generous and kind by handing out money even if that money is not theirs, stupid people will look at this person handing out money and assume they are generous not realizing it's not his money to give away? The taxpayer who is footing the bill has his dilemma, which can be modeled by a gaming matrix. Fight for principles don't pay taxes and go to jail. Or ignore principle pay taxes and keep some of his money. This is very like a robber who says give me the money out of your wallet or I'll shoot you it's not worth being shot so you hand them your wallet. Most people decide it is not worth fighting they are just trying to live as best they can so the average Joe ends up paying the bill and keeping his mouth shut and try not to think too much about it. By doing this the tax payer is doing what profits him. Everyone does what profits him the most. There is no interaction between people in which each person doesn't try to maximize their own profit. And gaming theory shows this to be the case.

I have asked students in my zoology classes to bring to my attention any example anywhere in the entire animal kingdom that does not follow gaming theory. I have never had a student yet find an example even with the reward of an A for the entire course offered. In many open class discussions, I have yet to find a case of an organism doing acts that hurt it and help another. This is a good leading into the next chapter called profit motive.

Chapter 4
Profit Motive

The concept of Profit motive it is very simple. It means any time anyone does anything, every roll of the dice, at every turn of the game, people will seek to maximize their own profit. In the game of life people play to win. Profit is the motivational force driving and explaining gaming theory. People will seek the carrot and avoid the stick. They will seek pleasure and avoid pain. Even if a person, a charitable, self-sacrificing person, a person working in a soup kitchen for little money feeding the poor they are doing what they want to do. They are doing what gives them the most joy, most pleasure, they are doing the action that profits them the most. If anyone would argue that they could be doing something that made more money I would counter with they enjoy the feeling of working in the soup kitchen more than they do the extra money. Drinking wine at a concert on that day it is less enjoyable for them than working in a soup kitchen. It is an interesting side note that many schools require community service hours as part of a graduation requirement. And many students keep track of their community service hours so they can put them on college applications. In America, we have many situations of token altruism. In America one of the best ways to make money in business is to declare your business a nonprofit. It might seem messed up to people that the NFL a huge profit-making business is incorporated as a nonprofit. However, after reading this book I hope you will see that there is no such thing as a nonprofit business. And everyone is out to make a profit. Everyone's behavior should now make perfect sense.

No government will ever create the best possible government for its citizens or equality for the masses, until they acknowledge profit motive and stop implementing any kind of government program without considering profit motive. People seek profit personal profit which mean they seek to benefit themselves. By understanding profit motive, you can see the difference between the fantasy of communism and the reality of capitalism. This is where the difference between the stable strategy and the theoretical optimum strategy becomes apparent. And it is the desire of this theoretical optimum payoff of 7 points per turn that continues to hook people into the fantasy that a big enough powerful enough government will do everything for them. The social leftists say it would be better if everyone cooperated and just helped every time. That way everyone could always average 7 points a turn instead of fighting and scraping for 6 points a turn.

But that payout cannot be realized because you can see this would be vulnerable to exploitation. A back stabber who would always receive help but never gave help would receive ten points every turn of the game. He would get 10 points and society would now get 6.99999 points or so depending on the number of those in the society cheated by him. This number is based on how his cheating dilutes everyone else's 7 points. You can see that in a large enough society small number of cheaters are not noticed. If the society or game was large enough you wouldn't notice one person cheating.

One thing that is worth noting is that in a small game his cheating is noticed swiftly. In a family, a cheater is noticed quickly, in a small group such a cheater is noticed quickly. But in a large society it is hardly noticed. And in a big government bureaucracy the cheater is not noticed at all. Until more and more people cheat lowering everyone's payoff to noticeable levels. And in large government run society's the cheater is so far removed from his victim though layers of government that he is unidentifiable. The thief with a gun doesn't rob you the IRS does on his behalf. And you can't fight the IRS and getting mad at the IRS is of no use.

The impersonal government can really take more from the citizens than would be tolerated in a more personal attack. This is one reason cheaters are tolerated in big government situations. Not only are they tolerated they are encouraged because the rulers of the large government aren't getting 6 points per turn like they would in a free market. They aren't even getting the 7 points per turn they would in an imaginary utopia they are stealing everyone else's points like a king and getting the equivalent of 50 or 60 points a turn. When you look at the average income of a lifetime politician compared to a worker it is more like several hundred points per turn instead of the average 6 points per turn.

In big government, the politicians i.e. the rulers are untouchable and the cheaters are anonymous and so both escape punishment and retribution much like a tapeworm who is hiding inside your small intestine is not noticed until so many of them breed that they bring down the whole organism. Government programs breed new government programs just like tapeworms. Everyone can tolerate one tapeworm it is only when you have a lot of tapeworms that the organism fails. Any socialist government can tolerate a few cheaters but they are all on their way to extinction as the percentage that cheat the number of parasites grows. This is one reason why family's, small organizations, small groups tribes or clans can be more fair and democratic and are more efficient than larger organizations. The cheater is noticed faster, his actions cause hurt quicker and he is removed quicker. However, in a big government of millions of people, parasites and cheaters are not noticed plus the rulers are untouchable which is a very bad combination. The cheating can go on a very long time since the number of resources, the citizens is so huge and the complaints by the citizens can cause no harm to the leaders so fixes don't occur. The problems will continue often until it is too late to correct without a crash. Another thing about governments is that the cheaters and parasites have voting rights so once the cheaters and parasites equal 51% of the vote it is too late to save that society. And of course, the rulers, the rich, the elite, will never suffer in the streets with the peasants so they don't care to make any changes to stop this from happening. Imagine if cancer cells got to vote on whether or not to get chemo treatment?

The examples of profit motive motivating all behavior are endless. Every single interaction is done to maximize the profit of an individual and to make sure no freeloaders benefit from another's labor. One such example that everyone is familiar with is birds. Thousands of different species of birds have complex courtship rituals. The male bird will have bright colors the brighter the better to attractive female. He will display himself on the edge of a branch singing loudly drawing attention to himself. He may not eat during this time. And he may have to do this behavior for many days. What is happening the standard answer is he is showing his fitness he is showing that he is a good provider and a good potential mate. He has enough resources to invest in bright colors for himself. And these bright colors also attract predators so he must be so fit that he can avoid predators while wearing an attractive suit making it easier for the predators to find him. He must have the best genes. He has energy to sing very loud which also draws the attention of predators and expose himself on the edge of the limbs further attracting predators that might kill him. This proves his genetic superiority convincingly. This courtship time for the male bird is incredibly risky but it is worth it because male birds who do not engage in such behavior don't leave chicks behind. Which is genetic death so he must risk his life with this expensive display or not have any possibility to make offspring. Male birds who did not engage in this expensive behavior left no descendants, they are basically extinct. Now why is the male doing all this? Because the females will not mate with him unless he does. And once again gaming theory and profit motive explain everything. A male bird who has put his life in jeopardy and invested all this time energy and risk of death who finally gets to mate with a female is very committed to her, and to her chicks. Once this long expensive display is done it is in his best interest to stay and help raise his offspring. It is selfish profit-seeking behavior to take as good of care of the female and the chicks as he possibly can.

Now imagine a Marxist bird government, the social engineers could say all this competition is wasteful. It is not for the overall good of the most. By the females requiring this long drawn out mating process many males are getting killed which is wasteful. And all the extra food the male had to eat to grow these bright feathers could be spent on the chicks. And all the extra energy used by the males to single the loudest could also have been given to the chicks. If every male would just not display and every female would just mate with a male who had not done any courtship everyone could get 7 points per turn

43

instead of the 6 points they are now receiving. Everyone could cooperate and it would be a much better society. So, all the birds agree to the new communist society. But what is going to happen? In the beginning, it works out great (in theory) the female bird sees a male bird and they mate and produce eggs. No long expensive, dangerous courtship, millions of lives are saved and the poor lazy males do as well as the more talented harder working males. There are no winners and losers anymore. We have equal outcomes and the gap between the haves and the have nots is closed. No wasteful competition and all the savings are used for the children as more chicks are raised. Everything seems to be fine except when you realize that there is such a thing as profit motive. The male bird and the female bird are both motivated by profit like everything is. In the past in the natural world each was doing what profited them individually the most. And that will not change no matter what government is imposed. Every organism will always do exactly what profits it the most.

But now the socialists have changed the environment. The socialists have changed the game so what strategy what behavior is best now? Let's look at what behavior is most profitable now. The male bird no longer has a big investment he has not risked being eaten by cats, hawks and other predators. So, what is his most profit driven strategy? He mated with a female and she laid eggs the most profitable course of action for him now is to abandon her and go mate with another female. If he can do this to 10 different females he will be 10 times as effective cheating in this new socialist utopia system. then he was before struggling and fighting to mate with one female and raise those eggs successfully. Even if half of his children die because struggling single moms must raise them, he is still perhaps 5 times more successful than a male who only had one mate but helped her raise her offspring. All this profit and it didn't cost him any risk, any commitment or anything it is a great deal for him. He loves socialism. Now it gets even worse than that. If he is going to mate with 10 trusting females who don't require huge displays of resources to ensure commitment simple math will tell you there must be 9 males who lose out. (this of course is just like in modern American society were 9 struggling middle class working tax paying families responsibly choose to have 1 or 2 kids because that is what they can afford to raise). But if so much of their taxes were not taken they might have responsibly chosen to have 3 or 4 kids.) And of course, all the children raised by single moms with no dad in the nest also lose out. Maybe the socialists in this bird society will hire more birds to watch and maybe take cheating male birds to court. Maybe they will start slogans like "It takes a whole village to raise a chick" Of course, they will have to hire bird judges and bird lawyers and bird police, bird jailers and bird counselors, and after school bird care facilities which all bleed off resources. Pretty soon this bird society instead of scratching and fighting with competition to have 6 points per turn if don't to a standard of living of only 4 points per turn. The lines at the bread crumb store are long and there is very little bread. And none of the common birds out of government get worms anymore. But all the communist birds just wring their hands and imagine the day if they can just make bird government big enough and do communist right this them they will all be able to live in the lifestyle of the magical mythical elusive 7 points per turn.

Is interesting that gaming theory predicts.

Repeatedly with 100% accuracy what will happen in the animal world and the political world and with individuals and with people arrested by the police and the world of nature and the world of human government. Because the situation of the long male displaying courtship required by the female birds is exactly what we see in nature to ensure there is no cheating and to ensure that he has a large enough investment to not make it profitable for him to abandon her and her offspring. Anytime a scientist wanted to understand what a government is really trying to accomplish all they have to do is setup a gaming matric and apply profit motive to the game.

Remember that every individual is only seeking profit and I will give another example to show how profit driven each individual is. Before anyone thinks that all of these long courtship rituals required by the female are only in place to keep these selfish, profit, motivated, patriarchal males from cheating. It might interest the reader to know that in some species of birds the females will occasionally abandon the eggs they laid because it is profitable for her to do so. The male has already invested huge amount of risk and resources to court her she has an investment of the calories in food used to produce the eggs at the point they are laid the male might actually have a larger investment in the eggs in the female. So, if this female abandons them immediately the male is left with a dilemma. Should he start all over and try to court another female risking attack by predators or should he just raise the eggs he has already invested in so much all by himself which strategy is most selfish, and most profitable for him to do. The liberal will say but oh couldn't they just both cooperate. Couldn't the birds just do socialism right. The cold facts are this Nobody cooperates, no human cooperates, no animal cooperates, no business cooperates, no government cooperates. The only reason some things look like cooperation is because the cooperating action is profitable for them to do so they only seek their own profit. And when it is profitable to stab someone in the back and betray them all of the aforementioned parties will.

As you can see, in any social interaction there is a difference between the theoretical optimum strategy and the real stable strategy. The theoretical strategy is the one, which will do the greatest good for the greatest number, if everyone would cooperate. If no one was selfish and no one saw or sought profit. Which is just like saying we could have a great government to govern humans if humans weren't human.

As can be seen all actions are profit driven all strategies in gaming theory are motivated to maximize the individuals profit. Any government program that does not take profit motive into account will not achieve its goal. The government that does this goes against all-natural law and all observable evidence. By manipulating the values in the gaming matrix, it rewards cheating and so cheating increases. In nature, there are no government subsidies, and there are no politicians selling fairness, kindness, charity, or bullying through coercion. The government changes the environment by changing the , rules and regulations of society and it is the environment which dictates the behavior.

Penguins are another single example in the endless number of examples of the environment directing morals or behavior. The Antarctica climate is so cold, so unbelievably harsh that for a single chick to survive requires both parents to be absolutely dedicated and monogamous, loyal to each other. So, this harsh climate has made cheating unprofitable. Cheating results in the death of your offspring so your genes are not passed on. Cheaters die, so cheater genes never get established in that environment. In that environment cheating is not profitable.

Which is different than the modern urban ghetto father who has 27 kids with 6 different women and the tax payers raise his kids for him. In that environment cheating is very profitable and he is reproductively more successful than almost any man. He spreads his successful cheating genes far and wide. As can be seen from these examples there is no single way to act to maximize your profit. It all depends on the environment which is the better behavior depends on what environment you live in. And in the modern American government and most European governments they have made one behavior much more profitable than the other. You must act according to the environment you're in. This is what causes a behavior to be profitable or not. In this way government policies shape behaviors and cause people to act the way they do. Because government policies alter the payouts of the game change the values of the gaming matrix and make certain actions more profitable or less profitable.

Chapter 5
Everyone, every Interaction is Selfish.

This might be the hardest chapter for people to accept. But I think it is about the simplest to prove. If you have followed my book this far you may be open minded enough to hear this observation out. Every interaction and every person in the world is selfish and only selfish 100% selfish.

A mother loves and protects her children because she wants to, because it benefits her to do so. Because she is selfish and it is the most selfish thing she can do, because she is acting in her own best interest. A father works hard his whole life and sacrifices to send his son to college, because he wants to. He does this only because he thinks it benefits him to do so. He is investing in his child who is more valuable to him than a business or a car or a set of golf clubs. He imagines his child as an adult and his grandchildren as wealthy and successful never having to work the horrible job he does or live as painful a life as he did and that gives him pleasure.

Mother Teresa is sitting with the poor in India because she wants to. She is telling everyone birth control is bad because she wants to. If Mother Teresa had ever said birth control might be a good idea for these women in poor countries watching their children starve to death. She would not be famous, and no one would have ever heard of her. The Catholic Church would have silenced her. Mother Teresa did what profited her the most. Through Mother Teresa the Catholic Church generated huge amounts of donations to feed the poor because people felt good to give money for this cause. A person giving $50 to Mother Teresa had more selfish enjoyment doing that than they would have eating a $50 meal out at a restaurant. It was a selfish act. It is also interesting to note that much of the money that was donated to the Catholic Church because of publicity generated by Mother Teresa did not go to feed the poor but went to make the Catholic Church richer. Mother Teresa was working and doing exactly and specifically what she wanted to do. All things we call good or noble or self-sacrificing are not. The person is doing what rewards them the most. They are not doing what makes them feel bad they are doing what makes them feel good.

Every single action and behavior is selfish as I've said before in over 30 years of teaching zoology, ecology, biology, etc. even with the help of hundreds of students I have never been able to find a single action in the natural world that was not 100% selfish. But the thing that the Socialists and cultural Marxists don't understand or seem to ignore is that if everyone has their cards on the table and everyone knows everyone else is acting with 100% selfishness the game is much fairer. The outcomes are much more equal, and everyone shares the wealth much more evenly. This is why free market capitalism has created the highest standard of living in the world. Although that is not a goal of free markets it is an unexpected outcome. It is ironic that the stated goals of communism are never achieved by communism but only achieved in free markets when it is admitted that everyone acts with 100% selfishness.

Another famous example of behavior which illustrates this point is the famous African lion their mating strategy is well known and fully understood to be 100% selfish. It is very easy to assign values in the gaming theory matrices and predict exactly what is the most profitable actions for a lion to do would be which is exactly the behavior we observe in the real world. These are the facts. Most male lions will only live about ten years. They are usually not strong enough to take over pride until their five year or six years old. As soon as they're able to defeat a male and take over his establish pride. The new male will go and kill all the cubs present in the pride those children of the previous male. This causes the females to go into heat and be receptive to him. He will then Impregnate them with his offspring. If he can hold the pride for 2 or 3 years his cubs will be old enough to survive and produce cubs the their own thus continuing his bloodline.

Now imagine a socialist, activist, liberal, communist, lion politician ran for government and lion society. He campaigned on a new democratic lion government platform. No longer would male lions be allowed to kill the previous male's cubs. Every male that came into power would let the previous male's cubs live. No longer would it be such competition. We would do it for the children. It takes a whole village to raise a child and all the males worked together to raise every male's children. Now suppose a male took over a pride that had several females who all had cubs. These cubs will take a lot of time and resources to grow to maturity. He would protect them as his own and patrol the territory of his pride keeping them safe from other males. It would be the best of all possible worlds for lions. And when he is old and another male lion takes over his pride that male lion will let his cubs live and spend his resources raising the first male's cubs it will be utopia.

Now a skeptical reader or a scientist will already note that this is not what we see in nature. And since mother nature is the greatest economist of all there must not be a better system possible than what she is already produced so why don't we see these peaceful communist lion societies. It is because they are unstable and vulnerable to cheating. Imagine a liberal communist generous male lion he has drunk the Kool-Aid and follows the party line. He accepts the politically correct narrative. At age 6 he is strong enough to take over a pride. The pride is a good pride that has several females and each of them has cubs. The new male allows the cubs to live, they grow eat his food, he must patrol the territory protected from other male's cubs use his resources, after a year or so the cubs are old enough and the females go into heat and it is his turn to breed them. By age 8 he is old and a new male lion comes in defeats him and takes over his pride. Of course, the new male lion is selfish so he kills all the previous male's cubs. Which brings the females in the season again and he is immediately able to breed with them and doesn't have to wait a year. The females have his cubs the first year. They have his cubs the 2nd year. And they have his cubs 3rd year. He has left 3 years of descendants while the politically correct male lion who followed the rules has left zero. His politically correct Kool-Aid drinking genes are on their way to extinction.

By the way this strategy is also true of male chimpanzee; our closest living relatives who share 98% of our genes. Chimps kill infants of a female even if she is suspected of mating with males from another troop. They can afford to do this even when unsure because sperm are so cheap for males to produce. It is interesting to note that this is similar to the behavior of many fundamentalist Muslim governments who are much more successful and increasing at a much faster rate than Western societies. This cost difference in sperm and egg of carrying the baby for 9 months or spending 9 seconds to produce it is one reason human males and females have a different standard of expected mating behavior. Just like the male lions, and for the same reason the male chimps can't take a chance of wasting resources raising another male's offspring. The chimps also cannot try a socialist, communist, peace treaty with all male chimps agreeing to sign a non-aggression Pac because it would be vulnerable to cheating. Chimps are not smarter than humans but the common chimp is less easily fooled than the common human. There is no way to make sure the other chimps won't cheat because in such a compromise cheating is profitable and any time cheating is profitable, cheating will be done.

The same is true of dolphins it is a documented fact that male dolphin's impregnate females by rape and kill baby dolphins that are not their own offspring. It is very annoying to hear the ignorant starry-eyed liberals speak out loud phrases such as "of all creatures in nature only man murders" this like so many other things the Marxists say is simply not true. Rats, chimps, lions, dolphins, ants etc. have no problem with murder if it profits them. One underlying principle that all life follows is to live and to maximize life, you must act in a way that serves you and not your competitors. This is also how dolphin society works, lion society works, chimp society works and each and every single society works that is not on its way to extinction. Dolphins rape because it is profitable to rape, they murder because it is profitable to murder. They will likely kill offspring of different males because it is selfish they are acting in the most profitable way possible.

These examples of brutal efficiency and simple economics are seen in the natural real world and the business world and they are certainly seen in every aspect of government. No creature can afford to do things that don't profit it and no creature or species or group does unprofitable things for long and survives. Often these behaviors don't make sense to casual observers but nature always makes sense. People might make a confusion out of the truth of nature but nature always makes sense.

As can be seen from the previous examples Which describe exactly what happens in nature, every act is selfish and if anyone does not act selfishly they go extinct. Because never will you get EVERYONE to not act selfishly. There will always be a cheater to take advantage of the system. This is one reason why cheaters love laws. Laws stop the law followers not the law breakers. You can tell the corruption of the society because it is directly proportional to the number of laws that society has.

As soon a one individual in the organization acts selfishly and they are killed for that behavior the selfish behavior will go extinct. But if that organization lets the cheating continue then that group is on its way to extinction. And as with the United States Government if the cheating is not only tolerated but rewarded the destruction is even more imminent

Again, I would like to point out that every interaction is selfish and everything is selfish. It's not just that the males are acting selfish and the gentle females must put up with him. It's also the females who are acting with upmost selfishness. Just like if there is a single generous male lion his bloodline would not survive and would go extinct what if there was a single generous loyal female who would not breed with this new male after he had killed her cubs. Her loyal behavior would put her at a disadvantage and would disappear from the population. Because her sisters the other females of the pride who bred with this new male would leave offspring with that same trait. As can be seen the behavior of the lion both male and female is simply the most selfish profit driven behavior possible. They are maximizing their profit in a gaming matrix. This is one theory as why human males and females have such different reactions to illegal immigrants coming into a society. Perhaps human male and female behaviors have been shaped over millions of years of evolution.

For the behavior to change the rewards and punishments of those behaviors must change. It is impossible to have unprofitable behavior increase when it is punished by the results of that behavior. So, if society is supposed to change or manipulate behavior they must make the behaviors expensive that they want to decrease and the behaviors profitable that they want to increase.

Now try to imagine a case where killing the offspring would be unprofitable for the male lions. What if all the females would turn on him and refuse to mate with a baby killer? In this case, the rules of the game would make killing infants unprofitable. But, the observed behavior is that the female lions watch as the male kills their cubs. They then come into heat quicker, almost immediately mate with the new male and produce cubs with him; minimizing their loss of the old male's cubs. Any females that mourn the loss of her babies would be less competitive than the females who wrote off the loss and moved on quickly. Perhaps that reproductive strategy has been tried in the past and was unstable. All it would take is 9 loyal good females to not mate with the baby killer and one disloyal cheating female to mate with him to destroy the entire system. Because it would profit that one female to cheat and mate with the baby killer and leave copies of her genes into the next generation rather than face the same genetic fate as her cubs and sisters.

Now imagine a slutty disloyal female lion who happily mated with the new male lion who had killed her cubs, while her noble, loyal, sisters refused to mate with the baby killer. The noble, stoic line would go extinct while the line of the disloyal female lions who ignored their cub's deaths and quickly mated with the baby killer would increase. They would produce more offspring and they would be at a huge advantage because the loyal mothers not having cubs would leave more food and resources for the new cubs that the baby killing male lion and the slutty female lions made. It is interesting that this is exactly what we see in nature. It is also interesting to note that this exact same thing probably happened countless times in human history and prehistory among warring tribes and nations.

The male lions and the female lions are both simply maximizing their profit. There is simply no other way for lions to act unless the environment in Africa suddenly drastically changed which would change the input weights of all the variables in the gaming theory matrix. Anyone with a brain can see that any government program is only attractive to people if it stimulates their selfish desires. Every government program offered will only be acted upon in such a way that maximizes the persons profit so if you want to know the consequences of any government program you just need the sit down with a little understanding of gaming theory and see how every individual will maximize their individual profit acting in the most selfish way possible and you will see how the people will act and what the program will cause society to look like.

As can be seen every single act by any living organism is selfish. This is also true of human beings no matter how well they disguise it. Humans being the

56

brainiest animals are very clever and complex at hiding it but it exists. No matter how many layers of diversionary behavior are stacked on top of it. Every single behavior, action and interaction by a human being is selfish. It is only by acknowledging this and working with that reality that we can defeat the monster. accepting that fact and making government policies based on that fact is the only way that we will ever get a good government where people are treated relatively equally and relatively fairly. It can be thought of as a drug addict or alcoholic whose only hope of salvation is to first admit he is an alcoholic or addict. If a person wants to break out of prison they must first realize and admit that they are in prison and if a people want to have a sort of fair good government they must first admit that everyone especially the ones who say they want to help the most and especially those who most want to be in the government and have the power are 100% selfish.

Even the most extreme examples of self-sacrifice are really selfish. If we examine each and every layer of any action we see it is just a selfish act. Imagine an extreme case of a homosexual transsexual who is afraid to come out of the closest because she might damage or hurt her family. Is she being altruistic? No, she is just maximizing her personal profit. For example, if we would assign a qualitative value to each action she takes we see it is to avoid the stick and seek the carrot. Suppose if she told her mother and father and brother the pain of hurting her mother would be 6 Units and the pain of hurting her father would be 5 Units and the pain of hurting her brother would be 4 Units. She would feel a total of 15 Units of pain. However, by hiding this from her family she experiences 10 Units of pain. We can easily see that her selfless act is really selfish. The same can be

57

said for every supposedly kind, generous act. If we really objectively accurately and honestly measure the outcomes we would see each person is only acting selfishly.

I work on a very beautiful campus which has about the most impressive grove of monkey pod trees still in existence. It is a beautiful scene with many other types of plants and trees all interwoven in a scene that could be a setting for a movie. Many times, people will sit under the benches or comment about the area. A friend of mine, a very sweet old Hippie loves to walk under the trees and she said look at all this beauty the trees all reach out their branches so their leaves just barely touch, respecting each other's space. And look how the trees make so many extra seeds more than they need for their own use providing food for animals. Notice how the white terns return and make nests in the trees and how these majestic trees provide a home and food for so many other creatures who all live cooperatively together in such love and peace and harmony.

It is quite amazing that I look out upon the same scene and notice how the trees reach out their branches as far as they can to maximize their profit and gather as much sunlight (their money) as they possible can. In fact, it's always a cost/benefit analysis computation for a tree to grow tall enough to maximize its ability to gather sunlight (that is the tallest tower to hang its solar panels) but not growing so tall it becomes fragile and breaks down in strong winds or storms. The trees must also calculate the building costs and risks vs the other trees who are in competition with it. A lone tree of say 20 meters tall is in an entirely different situation than that same 20-meter tree in a grove of 21-meter-tall trees. As they all are competing for the same resource sunlight.

58

My friend sees the branches reaching out to touch each other with their finger like leaves almost like they are holding hands. I am tempted to assure her that those trees spreading their branches out to touch each other so gently have all the love and care of a power company laying solar panels on a roof of a building and lining them up so gently right up to the edge of the roof. If you had a series of houses with curved roofs it would look as artistic and beautiful as this trees canopy. I also notice the vines trying to strangle and kill the trees taking their resources.

I actually did explain to her once that the trees were not making extra seeds at their expense in a conscious effort to provide food for animals but that the tree was just trying to maximize its success by spreading as many copies of itself as far as it could and bribing the animals to help. She looked at me stunned and said but the trees produce far more seeds than they need or will ever be planted and I said exactly. A tree must over produce seeds because so few make it. Much like a fisherman must cast 30 times to catch 1 fish and he might lose some bait on the 29 failed casts. She looked at me like I was speaking Greek and I realized that peoples lies, are their lives, and if you threaten their lies, you threaten their lives. And they will treat you accordingly.

She was able to look upon this very beautiful scene and had every children's story book fairy tale playing out in her head. And I looked upon this beautiful scene and saw the truth. An interconnected complex web of amazing beautiful. Each tree working with complex mathematical formulas to adjust the height to which it would grow to maximize its profit, each branch was growing at the angle, thickness and position to maximize its profit. The leaves touching each other and stopping at the point where battle with its neighbor made pushing out past that friendly/hostile boundary no longer profitable. This appeared to the Hippie as perfect cooperation and ironically it is the only time real cooperation which the Hippie, communist wants can occur. Which is when all cards are on the table and we know selfishness occurs dictating the free exchange of goods and services without government interference. Two men each with guns who will shoot each other for failure can cooperate very well. The most elite Seal team on a mission of death cooperates the best. While a bunch of unarmed jackasses with no skin in the game and nothing to lose cannot.

It is with my honest, realistic approach that I am able to see, recognize and appreciate far more beauty than my deluded colleagues who wear blinders all the time. I see the bark of the tree as a cost benefit formula. The flowers of every plant are a bride to attract pollinators some flowers are small and attract mosquitoes, some are long and must be pollinated by humming birds, some open at night and are pollinated by bats. I sit in this beautiful grove and see millions of meaningful complex interactions from insects to trees to mammals to birds in an endless cycle. Of conflict, profit seeking, cooperation and reality. The hippie basically sees a 2nd grade fairy tale. It reminds me of the story of the blind men and the elephant in which one grabs the tail and thinks and elephant is like a rope and one grabs the trunk and thinks an elephant is just like a snake, and another feels the side and thinks an elephant is just like a wall. Each only getting a piece of the puzzle and thinking that is the total.

So, to summarize this chapter the motive for every action by any individual at any time especially any interaction with another individual or even an interaction with an inanimate object such as temperature, sharpness of the rock, temperature of the road, every interaction by any individual will always be done solely to increase that individuals profit. If the rocks are sharp the individual will wear shoes. If the beach sand is soft and nice the individual will go barefoot. If the asphalt is very hot the individual put on sandals if the sun is too hot the individual goes under an umbrella or put on sunscreen if the danger of shark attack is great individual get out of the water every individual only works to maximize his profit.

The only reason someone like a Hollywood celebrity who has $100 million and 10 mansions and wants the country to bring in lots of refugees from Third World countries is because he will never see those refugees, they will never threaten him, they will never pose a danger to him. It cost him nothing to let in refugees, he will not lose his job, his neighborhood will not become less safe. He can appear to be very generous, he can appear to be very kind and he has zero skin in the game. But the people in poor neighborhoods who don't live behind gated community fences with security guards might be in danger from those refugees and so they are less likely to welcome them. I cannot make this more plain every interaction every action is dominated by profit motive there is not a single unselfish act in all the world that you can give me an example of. I hear old retired people living in Hawaii insulting and criticizing people in California who have children in a school district who do not want illegal immigrants to come into the school system taking resources from their children. Obviously, the retired person in Hawaii is hurt zero by illegal immigrate kids in California so they can afford to be generous. It is their best most selfish interest to say sure let in all the illegal immigrate kids. Its only whose ox gets gored. And no one cares about fairness or other people's problems. Its only when their own ox gets gored that people are concerned with a problem.

Even the person sitting on the board of a nonprofit charity is doing what profits them the most because they probably have a higher paying job than they could get in any other industry. I know many elementary school teachers who complain about their long hours and low pay. But I think, you are being paid above your market value. There is no easier major in college that would allow you to get as high a paying job with as many days off as an elementary teacher. I have sometimes said what job could you get that paid more and worked less? It is an honest question but that was when I was too stupid to realize that peoples lies are their lives. I was too naïve to know Truth is only a threat and insult to many people. The number of stories I have of pointing out the truth to people and shattering their view of the world would fill a book. But I can leave you with a quote that is worth repeating so I will repeat it. To anger a good man, lie to him. To anger an evil man tell him the truth. Another one worth repeating is. You can tell how close to the truth you are by how violent a person's reaction.

Chapter 6
Cheating will occur
Only when it's profitable

As can be seen from the previous chapter and I hope you understand by now, every act is selfish. There is no successful stable organism, organization, insect, reptile, fish, mammal, tribe, business, farm, that survives that does not act completely in its own self-interest. The reason we see so many actions which seem to be charitable is that they are really in the person's best interest they're not charitable at all. Those acts are extremely selfish but just camouflaged well. A farmer who took care of his land and treated his animals well and did not pollute his water out produced the other farmers around him and he was very successful. He was acting in the most selfish and profitable way possible although others would term it good. A tribe that treated its children well, encouraged the best in its people and cultivated its smartest best people and chose the best leaders who had the best interest of the tribe and not just their own selfish profit was much more successful and outcompeted the other tribes around them. We will see that everyone will do whatever it takes to maximize their own benefit. And when their ow and causes n profit is following the rules and not cheating, the system works well. In most natural systems operating in the natural world cheating is very unprofitable. And that is the point of this chapter cheating is not profitable unless the game is set up to reward cheating.

In Gaming theory, we see that cheating will only occur when it's profitable to cheat. Being a cheater or a non-cheater is totally dependent on how the game is weighted. If the game is set up so that cheating is rewarded and results in success then people will it's their only logical course of action. In a society where the rules are setup to reward the cheaters everyone will cheat and the best cheaters will be the most successful members of that society. But people who are not so good at cheating will be less successful in that society. Being a cheat, a parasite, or a liar is the best strategy only in certain environments i.e situations created by governments which reward and protect such actions.

Since cheating only happens when it's rewarded. It would be easy to set up a society where cheating was not rewarded and it's easy to set up a society where cheating is rewarded. Now which kind of society has been set up by the United States government? It seems apparent that in modern American society the government is set up to reward cheaters. One must ask themselves why does the government reward cheaters. And the answer to this is members of the government making laws rewarding cheaters are not harmed by the cheaters. It is only the artificial creation by Americas government that has made teen pregnancy, not working, illegitimate children, not feeding your kids breakfast, not being able to pay your rent, borrowing $100,000 to go to college, stealing from others, not taking care of your health, having a learning disability, being rude, going into another person's neighborhood and robbing their house, selling drugs, being a victim, etc. profitable. One of top examples of a behavior which the government makes profitable is incorporating. The government has created laws that give corporations more power and protections than people. For example if I sell a product and harm people I can be sued and lose everything. But if I am incorporated the harmed people cannot go after my house or personal possessions they can just sue (the corporation) haha what a joke. Now as a corporation I can do great harm and avoid punishment that I would not be able to do without the governments help. These behaviors are now rewarded by the American government and so those behaviors will increase. The famous case of Ford Motor company knew the Pintos gas tank could explode and they even owned the patent on a safer one. It was even disclosed during a civil trial that an internal Ford memo explained that Ford found it cheaper to pay off the families of the victims of Pinto fires than the $137 million it would cost to fix the Pinto. Imagine that. The executives of the corporation were protected by the government and allowed to kill people with no risk of going to jail, or frontier justice. It is only by help of incorporation laws that individuals can make decisions to kill people and get away with it with help and protection of the United States government. It is estimated that about 500 people died from pinto collusions who didn't have to except for the greed of protected executives.

In nature parasites are not tolerated the only way parasites survive is by camouflage, or some other deception. They must hide from their hosts and trick them into thinking they're not there. This is the same strategy and situation used by the current government. The current government must fool the people into thinking these programs which encourage behaviors destructive to the society are helpful to the society. One of the arguments used by the present government is that the cost of this parasitism is not bore by you but by the other guy. We will take resources from the rich and give it to you. We will take resources from this other race and give it to your race. We will take resources from this other sex and give it to your sex. Which are all just ways of saying we will take resources from the other group and give

65

it to your group. This is part of the deception used to sell a policy that rewards cheating. But the main point of this chapter is cheating only can happen when it is rewarded and tolerated and encouraged otherwise it would not happen. The decision to cheat is not an evil decision any more than a man who wants to open an ice cream parlor and decides to extend his hours during the summer time when it's hotter both are simply trying to maximize their profit and make the best business decisions possible. It is a cold calculated strategy. Different behaviors are simply optimizing return on your investment.

To repeat the example of the birds, a bleeding-heart liberal would explain that birds have the most violent, heartless, wasteful reproductive strategy on the planet. One that a good leftist, collectivist, globalist, communist, is should be able to improve upon. All the danger and cost a male bird puts into his display would be completely unnecessary if birds would just be good. All the competition, danger, risk, expense caused by these long drawn out courtship displays. All this could be saved theoretically, birds could take the entire savings and give it to the children. All males would have access to all females and it would be wonderful for all the birds. Except it these types of plans have failed every time they have been attempted or implemented.

The point of this chapter is very simple. Cheating will occur if and only if the game is set up to reward cheating. Whatever action is rewarded will be done. Pretending that people will not do the most beneficial action to get the most points in a game is foolish or dishonest. I will give an different example in the bird world to show there is no good or evil simple actions that are rewarded or punished.

Penguins are another of the limitless examples of the environment directing morals or behavior. The Antarctica climate is so cold and so harsh that for a single chick to survive requires both parents to be absolutely dedicated and monogamous i.e. loyal to each other and their chick. So, this harsh climate has made cheating unprofitable. Cheating results in the death of your offspring so your genes are not passed on so the most selfish thing you can be, the most profitable action to take is to be loyal and dedicated. Cheater genes never get established in that kind of environment. The male holds the egg on top of his feet so the cold ice does not kill it. The care and dedication and altruism and kindness and self-sacrifice displayed by penguins raising a baby would put other birds to shame. But it's not because they are good it's because that's the only way that works in that environment. Which is to say the values assigned in that gaming matrix.

Now imagine a huge climate change with global warming and penguins are thrown into a multicultural society as many birds from previously warmer regions move into their environment. Penguins project their moral code on to these new comer birds and as the climate is now warmer and conditions wealthier these new birds with a different breeding strategy breed as many trusting penguin females as they possible can leaving them to raise the chicks on their own. The penguins with such established behavior are now in the wrong environment for the behavior and will go extinct.

Think about the modern urban ghetto father who has 27 kids with 6 different women and the tax payers raise his kids for him. It is interesting to see that the more poor a society is, the less it can tolerate cheating, the less they can tolerate parasites.

Parasites or cheaters in a harsh environment will destroy the whole society but if you have a mechanized modern society where food is an abundance. In fact, the greatest problem with food is there so much that people are obese and die from overabundance of food heart attack, stroke, high blood pressure, diabetes, are now called lifestyle diseases. Half the people in the society eat so much that they die early from wealth. Well in such a society so wealthy and rich giving away free food is not a problem. It really doesn't cost the other members anything. Nobody in such a rich society goes hungry because the person who doesn't work for their food gets their food free food. And in a very rich society you could layer in between 4 or 5 extra people handing out the free food the welfare worker, the food bank operator, the lady who prints the welfare card, the bureaucrat who runs the office, the social worker etc. the very richest government can afford to bypass straight charity and make it so much less efficient. So inefficient that every dollar of tax money to feed the poor only 10 cents goes to feed the poor. It also removes the recipient from the giver so it never actually seems that you open your wallet and buy the food and handed it to them yourself. It is so well camouflaged that you really don't understand what is being taken from you any more than a dog understands the tapeworm is taking from him.

This is also why the phrase the road to hell is paved with good intentions is so accurate. Although I question if any government do-gooder really has good intentions. Examples are literacy programs, war on poverty, war on drugs, war on teen pregnancy, war on violence, social programs, welfare, school lunch, public schools war on homelessness etc. All these dismal failures were predictable if anyone had a clear basic understanding of human nature, gaming theory, profit motive, cost benefit analysis. You cannot make it profitable to cheat and not have cheating occur. This is the most elementary concept that people don't seem to understand. Every organization that requires life or death seriousness makes cheating nearly impossible. In fact, there are many organizations that are very efficient and effective and fair that work very well and all of them have one thing in common they make cheating very unprofitable.

One example of an organization that was very efficient was pirates. Pirates had an incredibly difficult job. Pirate ships worked in a very hostile environment outnumbered and outgunned. If the Pirates are caught they were tortured by awful means and killed, they were doing illegal activity with entire countries against them, multiple ships from multiple navies searched them out to destroy them. Pirates worked in very harsh conditions and had to produce results. If you want to consider the mindset of a pirate there are many examples found in museums and the Internet today it is called the pirate code. If you look at several different pirate codes most of them are very similar. Each pirate when he joins the crew and boarded the ship had to agree to and sign this code of conduct. It was an ironclad contract witnessed agreed to and signed in public by all. Here is a generic list of the articles of piracy I compiled and I think I did a fair job averaging out this from many of the different codes I have seen in producing this generic Pirate Code.
If you wish to see specific ones look them up on the Internet. But this will give you a good idea of what they look like.

1. Every man shall obey civil command; the captain shall have on full share and a half in all prizes. The Master, Carpenter, Boatswain, and Gunner shall have one share and quarter.
2. If any man shall offer to run away, or keep any secret from the Company, he shall be marooned with one bottle of powder, one bottle of Water, one small Arm, and shot.
3. If any Man shall steal anything in the Company, or game, to the value of a piece of Eight, he shall be Marooned or shot.
No person to game at cards or dice for money.
4. If at any Time we should meet at another Marrooner (that is, Pirate) that man shall sign his Articles without Consent of our Company, shall suffer such Punishment as the Captain and Company shall think fit.
5. That a man that shall strike another, whilst these Articles are in force, shall receive Moses's Law (that is 40 Stripes lacking one) on the bare back.
6. That Man that shall snap his Arms, or smoke Tobacco in the Hold, without cap to his Pipe, or carry a candle lighted without lantern, shall suffer the same Punishment as in the former Article.
7. That Man that shall not keep his Arms clean, fit for an Engagement, or neglect his Business, shall be cut off from his Share, and suffer such other Punishment as the Captain and Company shall think fit.
8. If any man shall lose a joint in time of Engagement, shall have 400 Pieces of Eight: if a limb, 800.
9. If at any time, you meet with a prudent Woman, that Man that offers to meddle with her, without her Consent, shall suffer Death.

These Articles were drawn up and the whole crew signed them in agreement, Captains were elected, and rules followed by all. If you look at the pirate code you will notice several things. First the captain doesn't get twice as much as anyone else. This contrasts starkly with the modern CEO who might get paid 1000 times more than the lowest paid member of his company. That type of disparity was imaginable a few years ago. I have read several Pirate codes and some have the captain earning 1 ½ times as much as the basic crew and some have them earning twice as much but I have never seen an article pf piracy in which the captain earned more than twice as much as his men. That single fact alone causes an entire paradigm shift in an organization, or a government or a society. Imagine a government where the president only made twice as much as the average worker and only lived in a house twice as nice and ate the same food. Imagine if every member of Congress only earned 50% more than the common workers he was representing and making laws for. What if every congressman and every politician had to live on Social Security and had the exact same neighborhoods, pension plans, medical insurance and police protection that the average citizen they supposedly represent had? If we use the rule of: Follow the money we can see it does not all go to the Caption in the pirate code. Also notice it says obey civil command of the captain it does not say uncivil commands of the captain. The captain was expected to give only civil commands. The other thing you should notice in the previous nine articles of piracy. The nine points agreed to live and die by for these men who risk their lives was that they were all very concerned with anyone cheating. This code is set up to be stable. Which it needed to be in a very unstable brutal deadly serious business. Nothing that has to accomplish real results can be unstable. The first article makes sure the captain doesn't earn more than twice as much as any of his men. The second article make sure no one abandons the organization. The third article make sure no one steals from the organization. The fourth article make sure anyone meeting with a thief from a different organization will treat him poorly. The fifth article make sure no one will strike another while on the boat. Most of those articles said fights would be settled on shore with gun or swords in a fair manner witnessed by all parties. The sixth article make sure no one will smoke or have an open fire by the gunpowder thus threatening the whole ship. If you smoked you did it on deck not below etc. The seventh article make sure every pirate is always ready to fight for his fellow pirates and has his weapons always ready, not being ready to fight for your fellow pirates at any time was a sever crime. The eighth article that anyone who loses a limb in the fight will get paid for it he is not just out of luck. Now it might see this is a generous rule but think about it. This is a good rule because if it did not exist, it would reward the cheater who during a fight with another ship held back and was not so brave or did not risk his limbs much. That article is a selfish one. In the ninth article that any pirate that rapes a prudent woman will be put to death. As I looked many of the Pirate codes had that or a similar rule signed and agreed to by all on the ship. Since everything is selfish perhaps that had some advantage in reputation or not causing entire towns or ports to turn against the pirates. Perhaps it was an agreement to keep prostitutes employed? Perhaps it kept fighting among the men down? Whatever the reason it existed in most Pirate codes. As can be seen the pirate code is very concerned with making sure people, members of the organization do not take advantage of the organization. It is very similar to military rules, sports team rules, tribal rules or any time an organization needed to get results. In serious military times traders are put to death anyone who disrupted the organization and decreased its efficiency was put to death. Cheating was never rewarding when it really counts. When one life or death are on the line the rules reflex that. Cheating is only rewarded in soft decadent societies that are so large that the cheaters and cheating is not noticed by the individual. In fact, modern society has tried to remove any personal effect of the cheating so that no one really becomes angry about it. Even our courts say things like the state versus Mr. Jones even though Mr. Jones might have raped Mrs. Smith. Mrs. and Mr. Smith has no say in this. It is a crime against the state not against Mrs. Smith. And what is the state? A bunch of anonymous individuals who don't care about Mrs. Smith. The only ones who care about Mr. and Mrs. Smith are Mr. and Mrs. Smith and their family and they are often denied any revenge or justice or whatever you want to call it. In modern American judicial system, the offender might be on trial for years and my get off Scott free with no punishment whatsoever in fact he now has full protection by the government if Mr. or Mrs. Smith do want to take revenge and of course to add insult to injury Mr. and Mrs. Smith's taxes pay for all of this.

In order for there to be a stable society, one in which cheating does not occur you must make cheating not profitable. In is interesting that as whole countries banned together and hunted down tortured and killed every pirate it became unprofitable to become a pirate and pirates sort of became extinct. However, along the Somali coast we see a rise in pirates as international ships are forced to be unarmed and become vulnerable targets and no country will chase the pirates down to kill them. So as the rules of the game change the behaviors that are profitable change. People are always motivated to seek profit. People just seek the maximum benefit, the largest possible return on their investment. Now before anyone twists my words and thinks I am asking for a larger government with more power to punish the cheaters and law breakers more. I am pointing out that our biggest problem in American government today is we protect the cheaters; most modern liberals will agree the wall street fat cats and corporate fat cats are protected. And most republicans will say the welfare bums and people living on government payouts are cheating the system. But it is rare to get the same person to admit that both are cheating the system.

Chapter 7
The system is not broken

This is a very important point you must understand. The system is not broken the system is not flawed the system has not gone an error. The system is working exactly as it is set up to work. If you don't understand the system it just means you are just too stupid to know how the system is set up. Most Americans know that if America wanted to exterminate the Somali pirates it could easily. But why should the people with the power to do it do it? It really wouldn't benefit them personally at all. And it would be work to do it. The system is set up to benefit the 1% in power, not the 99% who live under the system. Why are people so stupid to think that those who set up a system don't set it up to help themselves. Remember the gaming matrix introduced in chapter 3 where if everyone worked and cooperated perfectly everyone would get 7 points per turn of the cards. That is not the goal of government.

The goal of government which is run by the top 1% of the population is for everyone else to get a fraction of that 7 points. Gather everyone's 7 points together and the pay its millionaire politicians 100 points per turn of the card. It is only through the government that people can be farmed and all of their points confiscated, taxed, gathered together and given to the privileged elite. The system is not set up to make sure everyone has their fair share

People don't understand how the system is really set up. I always hear my liberal, socialist, intellectual, elite friends the ones who live in million-dollar houses, who drive around in hundred thousand dollars cars with Bernie Sanders stickers, the ones who get to go to college protesting against the 1%

saying if we could just do communism right, if everyone would just accept socialism, if everyone would just work together, the system would work. We just haven't done big government big enough. The problem of the government is it's not big enough we haven't given enough power to the government. The system is just not working like it's supposed to because we haven't given it enough resources. I cannot believe the utter foolishness of this. Of course, these are the people who can't seem to understand in their air-conditioned houses and cars and medical care they are the 1% of the world's population and the planet doesn't have enough resources for everyone to live like they do. I don't understand the limousine liberal.

The system is working exactly like the system is set up to work. The people in charge of the system want to have as much as they can. The people in charge vote themselves big raises, they vote themselves big pensions, they vote themselves lifetime security, they gerrymandered districts so they never have to worry about losing their job and they all grow rich in the job. They will outsource factories to other countries because they have no care for the average American worker so what if this stranger who can do nothing to me loses his job? His welfare is not tied up to my own. It's not like we live by the pirate code in American government today. They legalized bribery in the form of campaign donations and lobbying. More than 99% of lifetime politicians become millionaires in the job that doesn't pay that much. The system is working wonderful it could not be doing better for THEM. If you can come into the system, be put in charge of the system and become a millionaire in the system with a pampered lifestyle it's working just the way you want it just as it should.

I absolutely cannot understand the people who think the system just needs more power and more money and be given more resources and then it will become more fair and take less advantage of the poor. I don't know if this is some form of Stockholm syndrome or that it's only supported by the rich limousine liberals who want the system to continue but I think the data shows beyond a shadow of doubt if we compare North Korea with South Korea or East Germany with West Germany during the Cold War or Taiwan with communist China during the Cold War. Or China of the 1950s versus China of the 2010s. We can see which gave a higher quality of life to the average person in that society or under big or little government.

Just like a leopard has spots to camouflage his attack or an alligator has camouflaged his back to look like a floating log. The system that preys on people is not honestly revealing itself or its true intentions. If money to help the poor find homes keeps the poor out of homes and goes to those people implementing the program, just saying that they want the poor to have homes that means the system is working very well. Those supposedly trying to get the poor into homes keep their jobs which pays for them to have their homes. It is working exactly how it was set up to work by the people who set it up that way. The world seems messed up and unfair because government policies have made it profitable or advantageous for the world to be messed up and unfair.

If the system was fairer and did not benefit the government but benefited the masses then the government would be poorer and the masses richer. It would not be as profitable for the government to do that. This is one of the most difficult things for some people to understand.

Government is not going to harm government. Nothing harms itself. Nothing gives up its own life or existence. The system is not broken it's not that we just need to do more socialism or more communism or make the government larger. It's not that the government must become so big that people can't cheat. It's that the system is working exactly like it is designed to work. If we want a different outcome we must change the system. No system benefits everyone and the system we have now benefits the government and the expense of the people. If the government makes it hard to start a business it is not because the system is broken and not working correctly. It is precisely because the system is designed by those already in power who do not want competition from a new start up business so the system is designed to discourage people from starting a business. It protects those who already have a business even though it must lie and deceive to make people accept this.

CHAPTER 8
It is a conspiracy

I will share a funny story with you that will lose some of the humor in the telling because you sort of had to be there. I had a good friend who was an extreme fundamentalist Christian. He thought the earth was 6000 years old. He literally believed every word of the Bible. He thought it odd a nice fellow like me who had a good family and was morally sound would think otherwise but he didn't try to burn me at the stake or anything so we got along even though he had radical ideas. He didn't think dinosaurs were real etc. Well one day he shared with me his conspiracy theory. He said; The government and all these commissions where plotting to take over the world, he explained that they were responsible for a master plan that was doing things like watering down the public schools and text books making the kids dumber and dumber. He explained how all the TV shows were pushing a cultural agenda, showing the father as worthless and dumb. That TV had gone from having TV shows like Father Knows Best or the Andy Griffith show to shows that no longer had a strong father or even showed a family. He explained how the show All in the Family was designed to destroy American culture that Archie Bunker who was the only one who worked in that show and supported everyone else in the family who had to drop out of school to work and sacrifice was always portrayed as an idiot who couldn't put together a sentence and mispronounce common words and was a buffoon in the butt of every joke. All the time the freeloading communist son-in-law was portrayed as smart and with it. He explained how every government program was designed to break up the family and get people dependent upon the government for food and safety. He explained how Christianity was under constant attack and holidays were secularized. He explained how morality and common decency were being removed from the public schools and training of the young people. He explained how institutions like the Boy Scouts and Girl Scouts and Little League football and father-son camping, were all being removed from the culture. He went on and on with many other examples of how there was this giant government conspiracy to destroy the family unit, Christianity, morality, how TV was sexualized and promiscuity was encouraged and people were taught to be shallow and trivial. How people were taught to devote their attention to silly things and encouraged to have decadent perverted lifestyles. How no one was taught to be patriotic and people didn't have to say the Pledge of Allegiance anymore and how people didn't have prayer in public schools anymore and how people were taught not to believe in anything anymore. All of this was designed to leave people with an empty, helplessness that would allow them to be taken over by an all-powerful, one world government as national boundaries collapsed and no one would stand up and fight for anything.

I said you're crazy in a friendly way he wasn't offended and laughed. After about 10 seconds of silence I said. Well you know that is exactly what's happening then I kind of laughed. It was at this time that I realized it doesn't matter if you think gravity is caused by a wave or a particle each will describe reality pretty well. You can teach light as a wave or particle also. I told him it's not caused by a giant conspiracy it's more like a garden being taken over by weeds it just kind of goes to hell on its own by entropy. It's not a plot by some mastermind alliance. A garden left alone will end up looking like a garden someone had purposely planted weeds in. I told him that it wasn't a conspiracy but I had to admit to him that everything he described was absolutely true. They I said well I guess it doesn't matter which we think is causing it we both see the same thing happening. It wasn't until years later as I put the notes for this book together that I figured out that everything could be understood if we just look at the individual profit motive. Even the individual weeds growing to the maximum height trying to maximize their profit and the battles and selfishness going on would exactly describe what you would see in a garden that went to weeds, just as principles in this book describe.

Another thing I will point out before I get to the real point of this chapter is the very interesting word conspiracy. Conspiracy just means a group of people are conspiring. Everyone knows this happens that's why we have antitrust laws. Everyone knows that if Ford and Chevy working together can stop Toyota or Honda from selling in the United States they will. Of course, people in positions of power will cooperate to stop other people. If Coke and Pepsi can dominate the cola market and not let any of the upstart brands like RC have a foothold in any of the stores it is to their advantage and they will do that. Is that a conspiracy? Yes, even the most ardent liberal understands that if you give all the banks power and don't regulate them they will conspire together to take advantage of the citizens. Well gee whiz what if you get all the banks and the regulators together will they conspire to make themselves richer? Of course. Oh, but if I get this millionaire to watch this millionaire he will protect me from the millionaire. How stupid is that? Every voter seems to understand that if Wall Street could, it would conspire and manipulate the market to maximize its profit. Funneling a huge percent of the counties populations money into a tiny fraction of the populations wallet. Anyone who oversees those investments and who could profit from them at the expense of everyone else would do it. People will conspire any time they can. Three winos in the street will conspire on ways to get booze from a liquor store. So giving all the power to three men in the job of banker is no better than giving all the power to three men in the job of government regulator.

Conspiracy just means people cooperate. Conspiracy just means people in power work together to get more. Conspiracy just means people in power make plans to take advantage of other people who are less powerful. So, anyone who asks themselves is there a conspiracy, is foolish beyond belief. Of course, there is a conspiracy people collude to make a profit anytime they can we are animals with brains and speech. How do you know there is a conspiracy going on? Anytime it is profitable for any group, organization, company, business, government, to cooperate. When people in a nonprofit organization devoted to homelessness conspire with the government to takes tax dollars and give them to the homeless for rent vouchers. Will a group of bankers conspire with the government to make banking more profitable? Will a teachers' union conspire with the government to raise teacher pay? Of course, they will. Will public schools conspire with the government to put private schools in the disadvantage? of course. Will private schools conspire with the government to put public schools in the disadvantage? Of course? Will a Police Department conspire to make the seizure laws so that they could take property from citizens who have not been charged with a crime of course they would?

This is one reason why the large and powerful governments are so destructive to the people because conspiracies will happen any time it is beneficial to conspire which is every single time. Government is nothing but a giant conspiracy because you have a huge group of people in power cooperating working together for the common goal of helping themselves.

This is another area I find so strange. People ask is there a conspiracy when they should ask when isn't there a conspiracy. 99% of the time there is a conspiracy which is just a group of people conspiring together for their mutual benefit. And the larger and more powerful the government is the larger and the more powerful those conspiracies can be which is another reason why large and powerful governments are so harmful. The idea that a group of people in power will cooperate and communicate to stay in power somehow being something only something aluminum foil hat wearing crazy people accept as a fact seems very strange. It is almost funny that part of the deception of the government is to brainwash, to indoctrinate or publicly educate its citizens through legally mandated public education to not realize they are being farmed like farm animals. If a slave owner could brainwash his slaves so that any time one of the slaves said hey we should be free these slave owners are in a conspiracy and this whole system is crooked that the other slaves would attack him. that would be considered quite an accomplishment.

You may laugh but this is not a farfetched analogy. Imagine the other slaves saying. Without the master who will feed us, who will buy us houses, who will clothe us, who would protect us from the other masters, who would govern us, do you want to live in anarchy? With the master gone not keeping the other slaves in line the other slaves would attack us and kill us it would be slave warlords and anarchy look at Somalia do you want to live like that? Without our masters in charge we could not be civilized. Slavery has come a long way into modern times growing more insidious and psychologically efficient. We hear the same arguments today. who would build roads who would stop criminals from hurting us who would keep her house is safe, who would educate our children. Etc.

If it seems like everyone is involved in the conspiracy that is sort of true. Government is set up like any other pyramid scam. Which is a business model that recruits members through a promise of payment by getting others to enroll in the business or scheme rather than really producing a product. As long as the scheme keeps growing all is good but it can't grow forever and so is unsustainable. Everyone understands this and that is why most pyramid schemes are illegal. However, if the pyramid scheme is so huge it can't be allowed to fail we have the United States government. It is unsustainable and grows by constantly bringing in more members. This can be seen by anyone look at the budget of government on any level for the last 200 years in the United States. This pyramid government scheme has 4 things going for it.
1. It continues to gain power and get bigger and bigger every new federal program brings in more people. The TSA agents in every airport are a good example of that.
2. The costs go up which means more taxes have to be brought in but like a pyramid scam the government produces NOTHING so it can't feed or sustain itself it is only a consumer.

3. It gathers members. Each person with a government job loves the government their livelihood is dependent on the government so they are now part of the conspiracy.

4. Everyone knows the system is broken but they are just selfishly hanging on till they reach retirement and can collect their pension. Everyone is waiting for their payout which is promised and comes at the end of every pyramid scam.

One example of this is the collusion between the United States government and the American University system. Our founding fathers were very sensitive about people being in debtor's prison. The concept that a person could owe their life to another by means of unpaid bills was a concern. Today we have laws regarding bankruptcy which in some ways seem almost too lenient. A person could run up credit card debt, buy an expensive car ruin it. Buy a house trash it. Put booze cigarettes, and other luxury items on a credit card max out all the cards make many selfish decisions and declare bankruptcy. However, if a person goes to college and pays a college money to get a degree and the degree is useless. The degree is in an area of no job prospects and the student cannot find work to pay off the credit care the government has changed the laws to make sure this person can never declare bankruptcy and get out of debt. This is an obvious area of collusion the University system as it does today could not exist without the governments cooperation. And the government has changed to very laws to make sure its citizens are in debt slavery to the system for many years after their graduation.

One important point of this chapter is conspiracies are not complicated. And people don't have to meet face to face and know each other to run the conspiracy. There can be a giant conspiracy involving millions of people all of them conspiring to bully manipulate and push their agenda and none of them have met each other know each other or have been given the official play book. One example of this is the politically correct narrative. Every person knows that they say certain things at work they will be fired if they say certain things on Facebook they will be banned if they put certain videos on YouTube they will be removed. Social justice warriors protesting and demonstrating in the streets and California and New York have never met each other but they have all been through the same training. It's a very subtle form of bullying, intimidation, indoctrination and coercion.

People are very susceptible to peer pressure a child knows the shoes and shirt and pants he can wear at school and the ones slightly different that will get him made fun of ridiculed and bullied. Let a teenage girl wear her makeup wrong and watch how the other girls attack her. Was this a conspiracy? The politically correct narrative taught in all great schools, all high schools, all colleges and all universities reinforced with laws and lawsuits is certainly a conspiracy in the same way. A Hollywood producer who wants to make a film in Hollywood knows he cannot get the money or the backing to do the film he wants unless it says the things the politically correct want him to say. A textbook writer or children's story book writer cannot get their book published unless it has the right message. A sitcom on TV or a news anchor on the news will never get their job unless they have the correct viewpoints. As can be seen by this. There doesn't have to be a full meeting of the teenage girls deciding what makeup looks good and who they will attack and who will not, it can happen very naturally and very easily. And just like that no one has to tell the politician or the teacher or the policeman or the politician or the book writer what they must say to be successful even though everyone understands what is required to be successful. The conspiracy has determined what behavior is profitable for the person and what behavior is unprofitable for a person. The politically correct narrative has now determined what behaviors get the stick and what behaviors get the carrot. And everyone with a family, working a job or watching a TV show. Knows how the conspiracy wants them to act. This was one reason the Trump victory was such a shock. Only in the privacy of a voting booth secretly casting a ballot could a person do what they really wanted without fear of attack by the conspirators.

Chapter 9
Government is Force

Government is force and only force. Government means coercion is used to force a person to do what they would not voluntarily do. In the best-case scenario government is a contract, or agreement among individuals of how they will be ruled. But that is only the case when a person can willingly sign that agreement or not. Most citizens not voluntarily join a government and have no zero say in the wording of the contract. In the simplest form, a government between 2 people each person would have an equal say and there would be a very good understanding between the 2 of who had power and what would be going on. It could be to prisoners in a jail cell and the stronger abuses the weaker every day that would be a very simple form of government. There is nothing in the definition of government that says submission to the stronger is voluntary or not.

The next more complicated form of government might be a family. A father and mother and 3 children. Again, rules or laws will be set up and followed according to who is stronger. In a family situation the individuals are codependent, interdependent and when one is helped they are usually all helped. The actions which benefit any of the individuals in the family usually help the whole family. Simple examples of this could be in the Pleistocene a group of hunters each working together to bring down a deer. This would be a very simple form of government.

The next more complicated form of government might be a tribe. In this case you might have less than a dozen families joined together to compose a tribe. This seems to be the form of government humans evolved under. For approximately 10 million years, chimps, gorillas, baboons, Australopithecus, etc. lived under such a form of government. Again, in this form of government every individual knew every other, no one could remain anonymous, no one could injure another without it being known by everyone. In such a group, any action by the leader that harmed the group harmed himself. There would be no way to take the fruits of your groups a labor without hurting yourself. The leader had skin in the game any bad decision by the leader that harmed the group could get the leader killed. In fact, being a leader in this model was a very temporary situation. Remaining the leader required a constant earning of that position. And the power of the group could remove a bad leader at just about any time. Even if you were the biggest, strongest asshole who could defeat any other member of the group you could not defeat 2 or 3 members of the group at the same time.

The evolution of government from this form to states, then nationstates, to nations then to super nationstates on route to complete global government does not change the fact that government is force. Government growing in size does not make it any more or less forceful it just removes the governed's ability to fix bad government. All form of redress for harmful government disappear as the government gets more and more powerful. Government has always been force. The force can be followed voluntarily or involuntarily, but it will be followed or the government does not exist.

In prehistoric family two sons could band together and decide to kill their father. In a tribe, four annoyed hunters could decide to band together and kill the leader. The thing that kept it fairer in the past and more socialistic was that the leaders had skin in the game. Their very existence was tied to the success of their leadership. But now in nationstates with huge governments the leaders are completely anonymous and can do any action they want, make any decision they want with no consequences. The leaders of nationstates now have the ability to take the fruits of the labor of all of their subjects and personally don't know any of them. And because they are so far removed and anonymous from their subjects and they don't have any interest in helping their subjects we know what will happen.

From a purely selfish gaming matrix we can see that they will act in their own self-interest seeking the carrot and avoiding the stick and make themselves richer and richer in their subjects poorer and poorer. The force applied by the government may be to cause great good or great harm. But this is also not in the definition of government.

Another thing I find amazing is when Leftists applaud when the government goes against the will of the people. Like opening the country to refugees. Saying that a government is going against the will of its people because the people do not make the right decisions and is really just helping them do the right thing does not change the basic fact that government is force and only force. Even if it is a force for change a force for good a force for what you want. How that force is directed and what is done with this with force simple how the force is used. A government is nothing but force coercive tactics, the carrot and stick but now the government has the stick and the carrot and the subjects have nothing. Of course, this will lead to many interesting predictable situations.

Chapter 10
Government is Deception

All war is deception. War is the use of force. Government is force. In order, to force the people to accept being bossed around and to give their resources to the government in the most efficient way possible the government must use deception. The greatest most efficient victory is the battle you don't have to fight. The government does not want to have to waste resources dominating people. The government is most effective when it can pose as a friend. A tapeworm does not hang outside the body showing the host that it is sucking resources from them. A leopard does not walk out in the open approaching a herd of antelope. A shark does not swim on the top of the water waiting to attack a seal in the wide-open.

It is a much more efficient government that deceives the people into thinking it is their friend there have been governments in the past which use brutal means to control their people and those governments are not very efficient. They spend huge amounts of resources on police and military actively intimidating, openly intimidating and coercing the people. A much more effective government would be one that deceives the people, brainwashes them as a people, fools the people into thinking it is giving them a service which they have not paid for. Our government and politicians are great at getting people to think it is giving them something they have not paid for. A government that makes people believe it gives them more than it takes from them has won a great victory in the war of propaganda. Even though any logical person can see that this is impossible because nothing can give back more than you give it.

That would break the first law of thermodynamics. It would be like putting in 100 units of energy into machine and getting 200 units of energy back impossible. But many people believe this is exactly what the American government does for them.

Everyone in the government involved in the deception must speak the politically correct narrative and push the party line. Remember no one can get into a position to influence others unless they have the correct, the politically correct narrative. Government is a conspiracy and all conspiracies work through deception. If the deception was not there than the conspiracy loses much of its effectiveness. So, this chapter supports another. If you believe the government is deceptive, it follows that it's a conspiracy for there is no way to have a conspiracy if it's out in the open and everyone knows about it.

Taxes are another form of deception obviously the IRS and the tax collector are a brutal coercive intimidating arm of the government with huge amounts of threat to modify citizens behavior. But considering how much theft the IRS commits it has an amazingly positive approval rating. Now imagine this. The serfs in Medieval Europe had to give 1/3 of their crop to the king and they were considered slaves. How many people in modern American when added all together pay even more than 1/3 of their income to the government?

I have heard people say taxes are the price we pay for a civilized society. If we didn't pay taxes we would have anarchy and death in the streets warlords would take over. I've heard people say the government does good things with this money. I even heard a person say it's an honor to pay taxes. No matter how unreasonable or intrusive the tax is for example the homeowners tax means you never own your home your home your most basic possession. The foundational home of your family is actually owned by the government if you quit paying tribute to the king they will take your home. And somehow people are okay with this. The homeowners tax is accomplished by fraud, deceit and class envy.

Part of the reason the homeowner taxes can be accepted by the American voting public is it most of them think there is somebody with a more expensive home a nicer home a bigger home who's paying more tax than they are. I also notice a significant portion of the voting public that do not own a home and may rent or live with someone who does own a home so as not biting them directly. And what is the homeowner to do one reason we have a homeowner's taxes because homes are such an incredibly vulnerable possession you can't hide them move them anyone can come around and assess them and if you kick up too much of a fuss they can take it away from you.

I remember being in high school in civics class and hearing about all the problems of the elderly and I remember thinking if we just eliminated the homeowner tax once a person had bought their home and paid it off they could live in it almost free it would stabilize neighborhoods. It would increase property values. It would give people incentive to up keep their homes better. It would incentivize people to think in the long term and put better quality roofs on their homes and make quality long-term repairs. Once you owned your home you would be very stable and secure. But a giant home that's visible to the government is too tempting of a target not to tax and it is the more hard-working, more productive members of society who have these homes so are less likely to throw up resistance to the tax. It is one of the sheep with the best which gets sheared the first. All government is force, war is just force, and all wars are deception. So, if it seems to you that your government might be slightly deceptive you have probably just seen the tip of the iceberg.

Chapter 11
Identify who Benefits

Now that we understand all government is a conspiracy i.e. a group of people working together to further their interests and make life better for themselves.

And we also understand that all government once it reaches a certain size is deception.

We must learn to ask ourselves at any and every government action, who benefits. Every single law, every single piece of government legislation, every single tax, every single act by the government is designed to benefit one group at the expense of another. There is no such thing as the common good. There is nothing good for everyone. If you take away money from those who feed their kids lunch and give it to those who don't you have hurt one and helped the other. If you shoot car home buglers you have helped one group and hurt another. If you tax a house owner you have hurt home owners and helped another group. If the city puts in a golf course some people are helped and some people are hurt. If you or your group is not clearly and directly benefited from an action by government then it is most likely harmed by that action.

This is a very important chapter to understand how government works. You must ask the question and answer the question. Who benefits from this government policy. Ask yourself who benefits most from this government law? Who is it designed to profit? Also remember all government is deception All creditors and all parasites camouflage themselves. A lion doesn't walk up to a zebra in grass as short and neatly trimmed as a golf course. The zebra would see him, identify him as a threat trying to kill him and run away. The same is with government, the government who wants to take from person A and give to person B and of course taking a large cut for themselves, cannot let person A know they are stealing from them.

It is a sad condition of human beings. The jealous nature of humans that a person is happy and accepts a dollar is being stolen from him as long he thinks $100 is being stolen from another person. Humans are so selfish and profit driven that they will almost always accept that. This like everything about humans is due to and explained by gaming theory and profit motive if I lose $3 and my competitor loses $100 I have gained $97 of advantage. Our human programming allows the government to manipulate us like that. Just like our desire for fat and salt and sugar have allowed food companies to manipulate us into eating what we find so tasty. In the past, our extreme desires for those tastes was beneficial but now it is killing us. And in the past our extreme desire to put our competitors at a huge disadvantage even if it put us at a slight disadvantage is now killing us. The government must always project the image that you get more for your money, more return on your dollar, more benefits that you pay out.

Of course, anyone can see this is impossible, no one can return more to you than you give them. And people don't even believe that most people believe government will take more from someone else and give it to them. They must do this and also take their own cut which makes it impossible to help the most people. But they give the illusion of doing this by soaking and punishing the rich. Steal from the rich. Which of course anyone with eyes who looks around and sees that the rich are not disappearing should note that is not happening. But the government like any pyramid scam must give the impression it is giving you something and you will get a big payout.

One example of this is protection, the government takes more taxes from you to pay for protections from thieves then thieves would have taken from you if you were just allowed to defend yourself. It is interesting that so many laws are set up to protect criminals from victims in American society. Now who really benefits from this arrangement? The government which like any organism, any entity, wants to reproduce, expand and grow so since the government's goal is to grow and one need of this is to have criminals to victimize victims. What If the victims rose up and removed criminals, the government would lose a resource of growth and power. It could be predicted that the governments job is to now make more criminals. Hopefully this finally makes sense. Remember Governments job like everything is to expand and grow. Government like everyone is 100% selfish. Government's purpose is not to protect its citizens so if more criminals and more danger make more government possible then Government can be expected to protect and increase criminals and this is exactly what we see. More prisons, more criminals, more laws to stop law abiding citizens from killing criminals, money given to criminals, tax money spent on criminal's medical care. There is much more money spent on criminal activity than there is spent on law following activity.

Imagine a government who handed a check to every citizen that went a year without a speeding ticket, a year without a police call against them. Imagine if the good in society were rewarded. What if that tax money was spent on law following and not law breaking. It is in the interests of the governments growth plan which is the goal of any and everything organism for criminals to be present. Government does not want society to run smooth that would mean less government is needed. Imagine if a city shot every house thief and hung them in the middle of the town square. What if undercover cops rode in cars baiting car jackers. What if women cops walked around with a purse hanging off their shoulder in bad neighborhoods and shot every single purse snatcher who came up to steal their purse. This would eliminate purse snatching behavior so quickly that the cops would not have jobs. Muggings would stop, armed robberies on the streets would stop. Judges would not have jobs; little old ladies could walk down the streets safe and unmolested. Who would that benefit? The 99% of citizens who don't hold any power in the government? So of course, that is not going to happen. The government is working just as it should. Government is set up to benefit the 1% who run it not the 99% who are run by it.

Many businesses create an artificial need and then charge money to fill that need. Therefore, it's important to see what someone is selling if you cannot recognize what someone is selling you will always be duped. Many times, society is manipulated to create a need that really does not exist. Is there a need for neck ties, do men need to wear ties? No not really. Business men could do all their work without wearing a tie or a suit or cuff links but realize culture through advertising has created a need for hundreds or thousands of dollars of completely needless accessories that contribute zero to rendering of service. Do women really need to wear 100 or $200 shoes to look good? No, who benefits from this situation certainly not the women who buy those shoes. But if the women don't buy those shoes and wear them they will be ridiculed by other women. It must be a conspiracy right. How do all the women know what shoes are in style and which are not was there a big secret meeting? This situation seems to make no sense but remember the driving force of any organization any business is profit not service. If a lawn care company could sell you dandelions then they would. If a police state wants to increase their power, profit, control, influence it does them no good to accomplish their goals making people's lives safer or of letting people make their lives safer. It is the police states best interest to make life as dangerous and unsure as possible. Therefore, if it seems like the laws of America protect the criminal and punish the law-abiding citizen. It might be because they do. The criminals keep the government in business. The citizens may pay the bills which often makes the citizens believe they control the government this is as foolish as saying a mugger's victim controls the mugger because he pays him. The government must protect its reason for existence, its reason for expansion, its cause of growth.

One of the most obvious example of this many people have experienced is professional development. Many companies put professional development days in a work schedule but I was always perplexed by the fact these experts never solved the problem they were paid to solve. In fact, they never touched the problem. Not only did they never solved the problem it seemed that everyone knew the problem was never solved by these experts. For one thing, the people in the organization spent the organizations money and so it didn't hurt them or cost them anything to have this professional development. And to not have it would have drawn attention to themselves. So, the cheapest easiest thing for them to do was spend other people's money and hire professional development experts who they would not hire if they were spending their own money. After a while I also realized that many of the people doing the professional development, many of the experts, the consultants brought in were friends of the CEO of the company and they would eventually be paid back by the company they hired even getting jobs as consultants themselves. One guy had given favors for 15 years to consultants and expected those favors to be returned once he retired. When I applied this principle to the question. Why are we not solving the problem? Well the answer is simple it is not profitable to solve the problem. But it is profitable to the consultants, experts and professional developers to have a problem without a problem they make no money.

Think about this if the highly-paid problem solvers really solved the problems they would end up like the Irish wolfhounds who having killed all the wolves in Ireland were of no longer any use and went extinct. Why would intelligent people who are paid a lot of money. To solve a problem, want that problem gone. If the problem is gone there is no need of them they make their money on that problem existing if the problems gone they're gone which is exactly what the Irish wolfhounds did and those people are much smarter and much sneakier than a dog.

Chapter 12
Identify who is Harmed

To truly understand government, you must not only be able to ask and answer accurately who is helped by an action you must also be able to identify who is harmed. Being able to identify who is harmed in any interaction will allow you to understand why government policies, laws, don't seem to make much sense on a surface level. You must quit looking at government through the distorted lens of, government is there to help you. Every action is selfish and every action by government is selfish. There is an old saying" The closest to immortality is a temporary government program". That is because as soon as a government program is instituted doing away with that government program hurts someone from the government. Any change in the laws harms someone making a living from that law. Imagine how many people careers harmed if marijuana was made legal. Imagine the lost revenue and power of the police departments, judges, lawyers, rehab etc. Look at the Department of Education millions of careers are made from that department high-paying careers with short work schedules, good insurance benefits and wonderful retirement plans. Any threat to that would harm a great deal of people. Just as you should never ask a barber if you need a haircut. You should never ask a barber if you need to spend more money on your hair. Every person connected to the Department of Education thinks the department of education should receive more money and never be cut. The Department of Defense imagine if the United States closed all those spaces in all those foreign countries imagine the number of people harmed by that. So not only do you have to see who benefits from the program a government policy you must also consciously look at who would be harmed by changing, improving, streamlining, or doing away with that government program. If you drain the swamp a lot of snakes, frogs, toads, reptiles etc. are harmed a great deal. Just as everyone seeks profit. Just as everyone seeks the carrot and avoids the stick no one will seek to harm themselves. Look at Uber and Lift two wonderful companies that provide a service everyone seems to like. Who is harmed? The taxi companies who have spent millions of dollars lobbying politicians to protect the consumer from something the consumer doesn't want to be protected from. It used to be getting a taxi was a difficult chore, it was expensive, complex, and the service was bad. Now people float into an airport or a strange city and don't even worry about renting a car they know they can Uber around the city with no problem. Now who could be hurt by this it seems to help everyone. The taxi companies, the car rental companies are hurt by this so who is going to fight them. But how can one corporation fight another only with the help of the United States government. Companies, corporations can use the government to attack the other company and consumer. Now Uber and Lift cannot operate in many municipal airports in American. The citizens who want the services have to walk out of the airport and go around to meet another citizen for a voluntary exchange of goods and services despite the government interference. One of the jokes about how corrupt our government is starts with the line. Why do people spend $200 million to get a job that pays $200 thousand? Obviously, it is because every politician becomes a millionaire while they are in office. And to change the system would harm a great number of politicians and so they will work very hard to protect the system that has made them so rich and powerful.

This way of looking at the government. Always asking yourself who is harmed makes you realize that government is nothing but deception. Just like a leopard must camouflage itself in a tree to prey upon an antelope. A politician in cooperation with an established business will prey on citizens. Only a fool would think the government will cooperate with a poor working person who has no money nothing to give the government. The government must always mask its true intentions because it is in business for itself. A person could go through the entire list of laws and ask who is helped and who is hurt and get a clear understanding of the history of law. Examples of this are like everything endless. A state that has lawyers practice law in its state will make a law saying no lawyer from another state can practice law in that state. Now is this to help the customer, is this to make justice cheaper and more accessible to everyone, is this to help make society better and fairer, no. It is to protect a privileged group that is in conspiracy or cooperation which with the government. It's only to help the lawyers of that home state, and an intelligent reader with an understanding of gaming theory will realize that this must hurt everyone else. It harms the out-of-state lawyers, and it harms anyone who needs to buy services from a lawyer. A drug company that sells medication to people who might use marijuana instead is going to spend resources to stop people from having an option. It benefits them to make the choice of marijuana illegal. This is not done to help citizens, this is done like all actions to help the profit of the company. Lawyers have the unusual position in that they live by the laws and are often in the position to make the laws, so we have laws of the lawyers by the lawyers and for the lawyers. If you want to see who the system is designed to benefit, to profit, just follow the flow of money. Who does the money flow to. Who profits? And who is harmed?

When one looks at government this way, with the question in mind who is being harmed it changes everything. You can now see why nothing in government will voluntarily be improved because any change in an archaic, ineffective, or even damaging, program harms someone i.e. costs them money, costs them their job, costs them their retirement, costs them their pension. So many people are dependent on the status quo in the continuation of the way things are that nothing that reduces waste or gets rid of an un-fair practice will be tolerated. Even the pawns living on the pyramid scam will fight to keep the pyramid scam going, if even for a few more years.

Once I had high hopes for driverless cars. I thought, imagine a society where no one actually owns a car but anytime they want to go anywhere they just pulled out their smart phone and call the robot Uber car. Now these robot Ubers would be so much better than the human driven Ubers we have now. The robot cars would just be parked on the streets waiting to pick anyone up, at any time, they never have to go home, eat lunch, go the bathroom get sick, take a holiday, be in a bad mood, or find a parking spot. A person could just go online and ask for a ride 24 hours a day. Once the driverless cars became standard an efficient network would become standard. The safety of all these driverless robot cars waiting for riders in the high use neighborhoods all accounted for. All the cars would know each other's position which would drop accidents to nearly zero. Imagine the advantages of this society.

1. No one would have to buy a car
2. No one would have to buy car insurance.
3. No one would have to do maintenance to their car
4. No one would need to get a driver's license
5. No one would have a job at the DMV
6. No one would have to register their car
7. No one would have to safety inspect their car
8. People could get rides quickly anywhere they wanted
9. Safety would vastly improve the number of car accidents would drop dramatically we would save 50,000 lives a year
10. The emergency room and hospital visits would drop
11. General insurance costs for healthcare would drop
12. The elderly would have better access
13. Parking lots would not be needed, all the prime real estate in cities would be freed up
14. Garage space in homes could be used for other things.
15. Highway traffic and congestion would be reduced greatly
16. Fuel consumption would be cut in half as rides are shared and vans and mini vans do routes.
17. No more drunk or impaired driving
18. No more road blocks, or police check points.
19. No more traffic jams

Why isn't this technology with so many advantages in place today? Well you must ask yourself who would it hurt? It would hurt a huge number of people. All the car manufacturers selling Mustangs, Camaros, Hummers, macho muscle cars, sexy sports cars. Imagine all the car manufactures BMW, Chevy, Chrysler, Dodge, Ford, Honda, Jaguar, Mazda, Nissan, Porsche, Subaru, Toyota, Volkswagen, the list goes on and on of giant multibillion dollar car companies. 99%

of the cars these companies manufacture would be obsolete. The United States Postal Service uses a postal truck a single model. It has a four-cylinder engine designed in the 1970s it is really boring. The body of the postal truck is a Chevy S-10 pickup with modifications. That's all there is, when those trucks need service there is one oil filter, one kind of spark plug, one kind of distributor, one kind of belts, one tire, one kind of hoses, etc. well you get the idea.

If the driverless robot car was allowed to gain a foothold in American there would only be a need for about 5 different vehicles in all of America.
1. A regular sized bus like a school bus or a city bus size vehicle which would run a normal on time bus route.
2. A mini-bus or full-size van such as a 12 or 15 passenger van.
3. A boring 7 or 8 passenger minivan.
4. A 4 passenger economy car.
5. A robot pickup truck for people who need use of a Pickup truck to move things.
Those 5 robot vehicles connected to the Internet just parked on the sides of the road waiting to pick up people and deliver them wherever they wanted would be the only 5 different kinds of vehicles needed.

Imagine the changes in America. 90% of auto repair shops would have to go out of business. 90% of the manufacturing jobs for auto parts would go out of business. All the tire stores which sell 100 different kinds of tires would go out of business. There were 100 different kinds of tires in all of America before robot cars took over. The price of parts would drop drastically. The shelves at stores would not have 100 different kinds of hard to find high-priced oil filters. No longer would anyone need to pay for parking, in fact all parking lots, and garages would be obsolete. That would have the benefit of freeing up a lot of expensive land that is now used for parking but also because those people, their jobs and businesses would disappear. Imagine all the land used in prime real estate areas in cities used for parking, all that is free to use for another purpose. It would also make road traffic much less. It would also put many of the big car manufacturers out of business. There is no need to make new model cars with new looks and a huge emotional appeal. All the engineers at General Motors, and Ford in their battles to see who will win between the Mustang and the Camaro and the Corvette are now out of a job. All the car salesman and all the car dealerships are now out of job. All the people associated with AutoZone's and NAPA and other car parts stores are now out of a job.

The police who write tickets for speeding and running stop signs are now harmed. With only 5 types of vehicles maintenance and vehicle parts are so much easier than they've ever been before. With proper maintenance which 95% of people don't do these cars could run 300,000 miles easily. Saving huge amounts of the planets resources. The real big issue is the safety issue every robot car would have the position of every other robot car in its world map. Collisions would go down to almost zero, no more car accidents, no more insurance premiums. The number of saved lives, injury, head trauma etc. would be an amazing difference. I don't know what the added-up cost of all the accidents, and law suits, pain and suffering and missed days of work and police time added together but it would be enormous.

1. Imagine the decimated auto insurance companies and workers.
2. Imagine the decimated emergency room workers nurses and doctors.
3. Imagine the decimated ambulance drivers.
4. Imagine the decimated auto manufactures
5. Imagine the decimated auto dealers
6. Imagine the decimated parking garage
7. Imagine the decimated repair garages
8. Imagine the decimated auto parts stores
9. Imagine the decimated revenue of police

Today we could have the utopia of driverless cars that I described but we will not have it because too many people will be harmed by it and those people harmed are huge and powerful and can give money to politicians so our society will not be made better because of the government, it will be kept worse because of the government.

Chapter 13
Identify what is being sold

Now that you understand in every interaction, every exchange you must look at who benefits. Now must you be able to identify. What they are selling. Everyone is selling something. The police are selling security. The firemen are selling safety. The schools are selling education. Although now we have reached the situation in which many universities are just selling a credential, a piece of paper, a diploma and not education at all.

Nothing illustrates gaming theory profit motive better than the American University system. A clear majority of students going are fully awake and aware it is a scam. I would guess that 99% of people going to college are not going there to learn. They are going there so that they don't have doors slammed in their face when they try to go for a job. If you apply a simple gaming theory box which could look like a tic-tac-toe box. To everyone, every time they made an action you will see each person is only acting in his own self-interest. Because remember everyone is selfish and does what they want. Even if it is work hard and sacrifice for someone else they are doing what they want. What profits them the most, what gives them the most pleasure. Some politician are even selling compassion giving the illusion of kindness and caring, which is profitable.

I've always found it strange how people can listen to a politician say he is going to give away tax dollars that is not his and people consider him generous. This politician has taken nothing from himself and given it to anyone. He is taking from other people and given to other people it is the most sublime sleight-of-hand in the world. And only a fool would see this and consider that this politician is a generous man. However, the politician is selling an image of generosity and people are buying it, and by people visibly supporting this politician they are selling an image of generosity and social acceptance avoiding the bullying and ridicule of the social justice warrior so they are benefiting. All government, all politics is deception. It is profitable and beneficial to pretend to be altruistic in a crooked system. To be openly honest would not be effective or profitable which may be one reason why no good man can rise to the top in government or politics.

There is an old saying, "if a man shall come to my house to do me a good deed I shall run from him for my life." This simply means most people sell their agendas by telling you. It will help you. Every salesman's class or convention or training teaches that the successful salesman changes the attitude of the customer from, the customer is doing you a favor buying from you, to, the salesman is doing the customer a favor selling to him. The salesman turns it around from how much of your money can I get from you to how can I help you or what can I do for you.

All of us would do well to remember the purpose of the salesman is to take your money period. End of sentence. If he could take 10 units of your money and give you 0 units of product he would. But by the same token if you could get 10 units of his product for 0 units of money you would. No consumer says at the checkout line of a store "This dress is on sale but it is worth full price I will gladly pay full price". Everyone desires something for nothing and everyone loves a bargain. They must act as if they are doing you a favor selling you insurance or a brush or a health club membership or whatever. This is another example of manipulation. Remember your mother might love you but everyone else is selling something and that is only if she has a large investment in you and because you carry half her genes which will be further discussed in chapter 13.

Many things are sold to us after creating the need for them. Remember this need can be real or imagined. For example, the United States has declared a war on drugs 85% of the people in jail at a cost of 30,000 dollars a year per head to keep them in jail, plus untold lawyers' fees, court costs, judges time, police time. Now stop to think how many judges, lawyers, police, social workers, counsels are kept employed by this war on drugs.

Who benefits?

What are they selling?

Follow the money.

Plus, all the other problems the war on drugs causes neighborhood destruction, lost wages, roadblocks, traffic stops, airport searches, drug-sniffing dogs' etc. These problems are not drug problems, they are only drug related because drugs are illegal. They are law problems not drug problems. All because the government is selling the idea that they are protecting you from drugs. Most people are too stupid to even ask themselves. Do I want protected from drugs? Is the cost of all this intrusion of my life worth the drug protection? Do I even care if my neighbor does drugs? Do I just want to mind my own business and live and let live?

You can see how the government has sold society on this drug problem issues. And they are charging a fortune to the American tax payer for a Service that most Americans don't want. Many social problems, drive by shooting, child abuse, stealing, old ladies being robbed we are led to believe are caused by drugs but they are not. No, they are caused by drugs being illegal. These problems are law problems manufactured by the government to make money for the government. We need more police protection; every politician sells more police on the streets but these artificial needs are a direct result of the war on drugs. If the drugs were not made illegal all those problems would not be there in the first place. People could stay-stoned overdose and die all on their own with no government involvement. But to the police and defense lawyers and prosecuting lawyer and the judge. A judge is simply a lawyer appointed to be judge he holds the same law degree and went to the same law school as all the other lawyers there is no judge degree he is just another lawyer. In fact, lawyers are some of the best parasites on society imaginable. One lawyer defends the drug user, one lawyer prosecutes the drug user, and a third lawyer the judge, judges the drug user and they all get paid. No matter what happens all the lawyers win. In addition, many of the politicians, legislatures; governors, congressman, and even most of our presidents are lawyers and guess what they do. They make the laws and of course these laws profit guess who, the lawyers.

It is interesting to follow the money and see who profits, common citizens don't make laws only lawyers and government officials make laws and they make laws to profit them. We have a system not of the people by the people and for the people we have a system of the lawyers, by the lawyers, and for the lawyers. The war on drugs is profitable for these groups. It is no benefit to common working people but they don't make the laws, they don't prosecute the laws, judge the laws, enforce the laws, interpret the laws, or any of those things. They simply foot the bill for the laws.

These groups get more money, have more power, all the things that motivate any businessman, by drugs being illegal. It is profitable for them that way. If the police suddenly said you do anything you want to yourself we don't care our only concern is if you attack another person but you smoke all the dope you want 90% of all social crime would be gone. The jails would be under crowded. But it is profitable for a certain controlling group to make drugs illegal. The government has more power and has more money if it is selling protection from drugs. There is even a term drug pusher, which is a big lie no one is a drug pusher. There is no such thing as a drug pusher but due to government propaganda everyone knows what a drug pusher is and knows what he or she look like. Drug pushers are in the newspaper TV and radio but they really don't exist kind of like Santa Clause. No one pushes drugs, no one says I have a whole house full of crack and no one to buy it. I have a trunk full of cocaine and I can't sell it I'm going to have to cut the price. No one ever said this marijuana is going stale no one wants it I'm going to have to do a 2 for 1 sale. But it is profitable for the government to sell this lie.

Everyone who can make drugs legal, who has the power to make drugs legal would lose everything, money, power, prestige if drugs were made legal. The need has been created by an organization, which is now protecting you from the problem it created. This is done in everything from the blue jeans you wear to the car you drive. Last year's model is old. Those jeans are not the right brand now. Those kitchen cabinets are out dated now. If everyone decided to wear army camouflage fatigues and all businessmen all agreed to quit wearing ties much money could be saved. The planet's resources could be spared. This would work until the new tennis shoes worn by the new kid in school and he benefited or profited by all the attention paid to him. It makes him feel good and important. This is part of the answer to the why do we have a "me" generation. If you don't know by now you are stupid. We have the "Me" generation because government has set up the society so that it is profitable to have that Me attitude and not profitable to not have it. If a society wants everyone to be respectful and it decides it wants respect to be common then they must make respect profitable and disrespect unprofitable. Just like in the articles of piracy a very clear obtainable carrot or a very tangible swift sure stick. Society, customs, behaviors, quality of life can be anything the Government decides it wants to reward and or punish.

Chapter 14
Follow the money

The easiest way to see who benefits from a government policy and to understand exactly what they're selling is to "Just follow the money". If you added up all the cost, of all the social programs and it's hard to find that cost because they're disguised so well. Welfare, food stamps, rent vouchers, free breakfast, free lunch, and Social Security. Realize Social Security is often used as welfare. A drunken woman who has 3 babies with fetal alcohol syndrome will receive Social Security. Those 3 kids will likely be on Social Security for the rest of their lives unable to care for themselves. In this case and many others Social Security is used as welfare but it doesn't get thrown around as a statistic as part of the welfare cost.

If you added up all the costs of all the social programs to help the parasites. It would be enough money to buy them all mansions and food for the rest of their lives. But, all the poor people don't have mansions why? Because all the government workers and all the other people who benefit from these programs the cost of administering these programs is sometimes 90% of the expense of running these programs. Everyone understands that there are many charities that give $0.10 to the poor for everyone dollar donated and your taxes are no different.

This is another reason why big government does not work, it is so wasteful of resources. There is no way for the government to steal a dollar from everyone, then spend 90% of that dollar on administrative costs, then hand a dime to the part it was supposed to help and that be successful. And of course, the 90% spent on the administrative costs provides lots of jobs for many people. These people do not want to lose their jobs so they must keep the poor, poor and helpless or they lose their jobs. If you follow the money you see how much money is invested in keeping the poor and helpless, poor and helpless. Who gets this money. Let's go back to the drunken mother who is never worked a day in her life nor done or produced anything of any value to society. She has 4 children with fetal alcohol syndrome completely preventable it's a lifestyle disease. Those 4 children will never work, they are parasites on the society and will never contribute anything positive to the society and they will receive Social Security checks for the rest of their lives. Or they may wind up in jail and still be costing society a great deal but only after they've destroyed the public-school system, state health agencies, and threatened and bullied many law-abiding citizens along the way why is this encouraged? Let's try an experiment and follow the money. Obviously, the children receiving social security payments get the money and the government employees who work in the Social Security division get the money in the form of their pay and benefits and retirement, and the construction workers who built the buildings and staff the offices putting phone lines and put on carpet all benefit they all received part of the money. And the politicians who now have 4 new voters who will vote them in office so they will receive the money.

As can be seen the number of people that profit and receive the money can be quite extensive. In the 2008 housing crash many of my friends worked in construction and they lost their jobs or had very little work. Some of them however found steady work at universities and colleges because of the flood of government money going to these institutions those institutions built all through the housing crisis so electricians and carpenters and drywaller's all got work with redistributed tax funds going to universities. Being able to follow the money to its ultimate destination will help you understand how government works. You can see it is a pyramid scam and many people are involved. They have a vested interest in keeping it going. Not realizing that if the government had not caused the problem in the first place they could have had equal jobs building things for people instead of the government.

Although sometimes it's difficult because like all good predators or parasites the government camouflages its actions as much as possible. Sheep do not realize they are being sheared, cows do not realize they are being milked or the chickens do not know their eggs are taken. Those animals all think the farmer has their best interest at heart is their protector and is taking care of them.

Chapter 15
There will never be an unexploited resource.

This is a very important concept to understand. After you have learned to follow the money and always look to where the money flows when looking at a government program, nonprofit organization or charity. The next step is to realize a law of zoology and biology and ecology that says. There will never go an unexploited resource. Any time in the natural world that a resource becomes available something will evolve to exploit that resource, it's simply a law.

There are many examples of this. At one time throughout Asia bamboo a highly evolved fast-growing grass that connection incorporated silicon into itself walls exploded in population it was the dominant plant in that area nothing could eat it digested a really take advantage of this resource. Then a bear came along now bear would rather he more nutrient dense food but there is this resource available and so the bear adapted and evolved to take advantage of that resource. The panda bear has incredibly thick muscular stomach and intestinal lining to tolerate the bamboo incredibly powerful jaws to chew bamboo. Bamboo is not very nutritious and the bear must process a huge amount of bamboo because so much bamboo is available and it didn't run away and it just was in the forest to be it was profitable for the bear to adapt a bamboo diet. Millions of years ago some bears started eating his bamboo and before long entire population of bears had evolved to live on the bamboo. Anyone can see the similarity to this and the social safety net created by the American Government.

Another example that there will never go an unexploited resource is on the island of Madagascar there is a lemur with a long thin finger and it is able to exploit and eat termites much like woodpeckers do on the continents. This resource of termites is being exploited by this specialized lemur because there will never be an unexploited resource. Termites were available to eat but no wood peckers lived on the island. So, a creature evolved to take advantage of to exploit this available resource.

The same thing happens with grass. When grass evolved there were not many animals that could digest grass but since this resource became available we had 4 chambered stomach's evolved ungulates who could digest grass. They can swallow huge amounts of grass put in the first stomach letting it ferment breaking down slowly. Grass like bamboo is not very nutrient dense and not a good choice of food unless there is a huge amount of it and it doesn't go anywhere. The examples in nature are endless. A resource that was not present becomes present. And something comes along that has learned to exploit that resource, to take advantage of that opportunity. Every opportunity will eventually be taken advantage of, by something or someone.

Hermit crabs are another example, of the law that there will never go an unexploited resource for long. These shells producing animals who died but left their shells behind, eventually led to an animal that did not use its own resources to make its own shell. Why waste resources and do your own work when someone else has already done it for you. (why do something for yourself when the government will do it for you) A creature evolved to use the discarded shells of other animals. Hermit crabs took advantage of an available resource.

Another example is the polar bear, why do we have polar bears. Well just like the panda bear is a mutated bear which evolved physically and behaviorally to exploit a resource or as science say fill a niche. The polar bear is just a brown bear but as the weather got colder and colder and ice moved down from the north a new habitat was created. One with seals and ice and snow year-round. Some brown bears began to exploit this new resource and split into a new species. No polar bears existed 200,000 years ago which is a mere blink of an eye in geologic time. There was no profit in being a polar bear from perhaps 250 million years to 2 million years ago. There was no climate of ice in the north pole to make their adaptations profitable. But as soon as it became available an animal evolved to fill that niche. The split between brown bears and polar bears has been so recent that they can still inter breed and produce fertile offspring. But polar bears and brown bears have radically different strategies, behaviors, and ways of making a living.

There is not a single example in nature where a resource went unexploited. Now this is a natural law that every scientist knows and understands. Yet the governments think that they can provide resources and nothing will grow to take advantage of those resources. The government behaves as if nothing will adapt to take advantage of the resources offered by.

The examples are endless if a free cell phone is given to someone than that person will adapt to get the free cell phone. If free breakfast is provided for families than those families will adapt to get the free breakfast. If money is given to single mothers, women will evolve to become single mothers. If not being able to find a job is rewarded and dropping out of school is rewarded then people will adapt to take advantage of that opportunity. People will always adapt to take advantage of any unexploited resource. And since government programs have an almost unlimited amount of resources they will encourage an unlimited amount of adaptation and exploitation. Now if you read the book so far you realize that these resources provided by the government are not provided by the people in charge of those governments. No, they are provided by the taxpayers who support those governments. Tax payers are who the government live off of. It is the taxpayers and the workers who allow the government to exist and so when the government gives things or provides resources to people it is only providing what it is taken from its workers. Again, this is where some collectivists will argue that a government is rich enough because it has so many workers who have more than they need that it can provide resources to those who cannot work or provide for themselves. But this is impossible because people's behavior can adapt so much faster than natural evolution. Just look at evolution it took bears millions of years to evolve in the panda bears. It took lemurs millions of years to evolve into the tools necessary to exploit termites like a woodpecker but all a person has to do is change their behavior. They can do that in a week. A government program designed to provide a resource can now be exploited by anyone who just simply alters their behavior this takes 5 minutes not a million years of evolution and so that resource will be exhausted.

This chapter points out the folly of a government that provides resources to people and expects them not to use those resources. It is contrary to the laws of nature for a government to provide high quality resources to people and then assume the people will not adopt behaviors to fully exploit and use those good resources.

Every organism will always find the most effective way to exploit the resources available to it so just like armor causes the development of the armor piercing shell, which causes the development of thicker armor, so welfare causes the development of the welfare cheat. Which makes a new welfare law, which brings about a better welfare cheat. Any new rule or law that is created to close one loophole is immediately undermined by 7 different ways to cheat. And the problem is government cannot respond to the individual quickly enough it takes years to get laws passed in the devise, to read legislation and to alter policy. Governments cannot move that fast. Once a government program is in place it took it years to get there and will take years to be repealed altered or changed. Legislation takes a great deal of time. However, an individual can see a law and figure out an unintended use of that law, tell his friends about it in the next week the entire class of cheaters are working the system again which will take years to be responded to by the government if at all. Because remember the government is not a person. It is not actually being hurt and so the politicians in charge of the government don't really care if the resource that they have provided is being misused or not being spent on its advertised audience. The politician who lives in a million-dollar mansion in a gated community and has a life time pension. That kind of man in that position has no skin in the game. He has no investment in making anything better for the common people.

CHAPTER 16
It's the environment

Just as there will never go any exploited resource, it is after all a law. Another law is the environment decides what resources are available and how it is most profitable to exploit them. The environment which provides or does not provide those resources will cause the behavior. The environment causes behavior. An organism's genetics determine the organism's ability to behave in different environments. In my ecology classes I ask my students. Is it better to be a reptile or a mammal? Is it better to be a flowering plant pollinated by bees or a plant pollinated by the wind. The answer I was looking for was. It depends on the environment. I wanted my students to be able to see that there is no single best strategy for an animal or plant to have. There is only the best strategy in a given environment.

One test question that I sometimes used is. Give an example of an animal that once was very successful and is now not successful. Or give an example of one that was not very successful in the past but is extremely successful now. One of the best answers I got was a student who compared elephants and rats. Elephants used to be incredibly successful found on a majority of the land on earth. The whole elephant family was successful. They were large intelligent, cooperative, long-lived and with their trunks and tusks could exploit a variety of plants on many feeding levels. Their size and herd nature made them invulnerable to many predators. Their tusks even allowed them to dig down and get water during the dry season. Their trunk and tusks also allowed them to exploit frozen areas covered in snow because they could sweep snow away from grass and eat it when other ungulates could not. The elephant family was so successful they were a keystone species on multiple continents exploiting forests, and plains, tropical and tundra areas. But today nearly all species of the elephant family are extinct or in danger of extinction. With the evolution of humans hunting those traits have gone from being incredibly useful to nearly useless. The elephants didn't change the environment did.

A contrasting example this student included was the rat. 50,000 years ago, rats were not a very successful species. They were not worldwide only living in a small area in Asia unable to travel or get around. They were very limited in area, they were not particularly fast-moving or mobile like elephants who could spread miles a day. They were vulnerable to predators. They would eat grass grains, the seed heads of grass ripened which was seasonal and not always available. They froze to death in cold weather, could not cross large rivers nor deserts. they could not live in a variety of climates or biomes.

But with the explosion of agriculture and humans the rat now is an incredibly successful animal. Whereas without humans around would not be very successful. There are towns in Canada where if all the rats are exterminated they remain rat free. Rats are not even able to travel through the forests and get to those towns. And those towns will remain rat free until some trucker or human accidently brings them. Rats could not colonize any of the islands in the pacific until humans brought them in. Rats have successfully been able to colonize the world in places they never could've existed without humans rats success is solely because of human help. Elephants could colonize most of the world without human help but with humans they have been exterminated for most of the world.

Both are examples of creatures whose success is totally dependent on the environment.

Dinosaurs are another example. Dinosaurs were an incredibly successful group of animals ruling over the planet for 100 million years. Big, active, warm-blooded, incredibly successful. But when the meteor hit Earth around 65 million years ago all the metabolically active dinosaurs died. And the only things that were left were the sluggish slow crocodiles, snakes, turtles, and tiny mammals who had been dominated by the dinosaurs. As soon as the environment changed a different strategy became better. From these examples, we can see that there is no best way of doing things. There is only the best way of doing things in each environment.

This is common sense. If I ask you what is the best way to play cards? You will say to me, what game? If I say to you know what is the best way to play cards, you will again answer what game are you playing? Are you playing poker? Are you playing old maid? Are you playing blackjack? You can't tell me the best way to play cards until I tell you what game it is and you know what the rules of the game are and what values are placed on what? This is just like human action. Is it good to be virtuous? Honest? Kind? Loyal? I can't tell you how you should act in society until I know how the government has set up that society and what values it has put on what actions.

The environment decides if an action is profitable or not. It is the environment which sets up the rules of the game and what the values are. If I set up a simple gaming matrix and invite you to play and we each are trying to beat the other and we each play one of 2 cards cheat or cooperate, betray or be loyal, help or not help whatever. It all depends on what point value I assigned to those cards.

In this book, I refer to a hypothetical value of 7 point if we both cooperate and 2 points if we both play cheat. What if I change the values what if I made it worth 7 points to cooperate and 7 points to cheat. You would have no incentive to cooperate or to cheat. And that would change the environment of the game. What would happen how would you play the game if I made it worth 2 points to cooperate and 8 points to cheat. In each case you would play the game differently and this is how the government by setting policies and laws and legislation is able to manipulate the environment of the society and cause people to behave in certain ways.

The title of this book is kind of misleading because just like there is no perfect animal in that I cannot tell you what the perfect animal is until you tell me what environment it is going to live in. Is a shark perfect? Is an eagle perfect? Is a cockroach perfect? Is a rat perfect? Is a worm perfect? Is an elephant perfect? Is a horse perfect? The answer to all those questions is. It depends on the environment. Is there a perfect way to play poker yes? Is there perfect way to play blackjack yes? Is there perfect way to play cards No. You must specify what game and what the rules are. You can't answer that particular question because you have not been given enough information. A child living in 1930 has a different way to act than one living in 2030. (I purposely am tempting fate)

With this understanding, we can see that the environment that the government creates is what creates society. The government is responsible for the society it has. And if you want a society of cheaters, of liars, of thieves, of bullies, of people who break the law, then all the government has to do, to create that society. Just create an environment of laws and regulations that reward that to encourage that behavior. By making laws and regulations in which that behavior is profitable. The governments create a culture of that behavior. It's all about the environment, and government creates the environment.

It is the environment that dictates what behaviors are successful and what behaviors are unsuccessful. And this is often missed interpreted by leftists who insist that all bad behavior is due to the environment. Sometimes the bad behavior causes the environment. And sometimes people who are most successful in a bad environment have those bad behaviors which fit the environment so well. Another thing is that without competition or any consequences for bad behaviors those bad behaviors can be very successful.

The United States of America has been a very successful country while having a less than perfect system. America has not really had any competition. Two major world wars that destroyed everyone else of any real competition but benefitted America was an unbelievable advantage, not a level playing field. Also for the few hundred years of Americas existence America simply had more stuff, more resources, more good land, more freshwater, than anyone else. Some states in America are as large as some countries in Europe. Forests of trees, oceans of fish you could walk across the backs of codfish, lobsters could be picked up and eaten by the poor, delicious squabs of passenger pigeons, 9,000,000,000 of them, buffalo herds that took three days to pass a single point, forests of trees for lumber, big clean rivers, fields of productive soil, huge petroleum fields, giant coal reserves. America in competition with another

European country the size of one of its 50 states was more unfair than a 7-foot athletic man playing against a 5-foot unathletic man in a game of basketball. Imagine after the win the 7-foot athlete bragging about what a great accomplishment he has made. Germany is 350,000 square miles less than the size of the state of Montana and Japan is 375,00 square miles. America is over 9,000,000 square miles. America was a fresh country a few hundred years ago Japan and Germany were old countries with used up resources.

The first point is that America really has not had any competition. The second point is that America is very young and has not lasted for a long time compared to other societies. Because of all it has and being so rich America can afford to be managed poorly and still be a winner, like a 7-foot basketball player can make mistakes have a poor shot etc. but still beat a 5-foot basketball player who is better coached and is fundamentally more sound. Recently some countries without the resources but better management are beginning to give America some competition. This has happened as the management of America has become less and less efficient and more and more rewarding of inefficiency. It also should be pointed out that America in the beginning was better managed than most other countries.

Once you understand how the government manipulates the environment you can understand how government encourages some behavior and discourages other behaviors. For example, I have seen multiple examples of an unpopular, homely, beta individual with no social standing among their peers, who suddenly became very popular and rose in social standing because they announced to their class that they were transsexual. I watched a girl who could not

128

get a boyfriend as a girl one year announce that she was a boy and now has a surprisingly attractive girlfriend. How can this be? A 30% girl who could not get a 50% boy, becomes a 20% boy and suddenly is able to get a 70% girl.

In our present environment, this is a very profitable behavior these people now have more attention and higher social standing than they ever had before. But 50 years ago, in the American society this behavior would not have been profitable. The government can create any environment it wants, and promote any kind of behavior it wants to. Do you want nice guys to finish last then set up the environment for that to happen. Do nice guys really have to finish last? Only if the environment is set up to punish nice guys and reward mean guys. It's really that simple. Nice guys finish last only if the game is weighted that way. One objective of this book is to get you to ask yourself how is the present society you live in designed. Which means who is it set up to benefit and who is it set up to harm? Some would say our present American society is set up to benefit the dumb, lazy, corrupt, the very richest or the very poor.

Is there a single universal strategy of behavior that is best in every environment? No. The environment decides what behaviors are beneficial or profitable, and what behaviors are harmful or costly. And the American government decides the environment Americans live in.

Chapter 17
People aren't good or bad
Everyone is just working to maximize their profit.

People are not good or bad. There is no good or evil. There are only two sides, each of which wants to win. Life is not good or bad. Life is not good or evil, life simply lives. If cows eat grass to live, does grass consider cows to be evil? I'm sure cows consider grass to be good. People eat cows, so do people consider cows to be good. Cows are eaten by people so do cows consider people as evil? Vegetarians don't eat cows so they consider people who eat cows to be bad. Some vegetarians will attack people who eat cows. The vegetarians who don't eat meat think they are good while the innocent plants who they eat consider vegetarians murders. Germs make people sick so people consider germs bad. A mother might put bleach on her sink to kill the germs. Do the germs consider the mother bad? People like all life forms simply do what is in their best interest in whatever environment they are living in. There is no such thing as good vs. evil. Only two sides, each of which wants to win, to maximize its profit. Every army, sports team, and serial killer claims to be on God's side doing God's work. They even pray to God before the game or the battle. There is not some universal good side. Only different sides each of which is ultimately selfish and wants to win. I have made this as plain as I possibly can.

People are not born good or bad simply because they were born on the wrong team. A person born on the south side of the city who hates the north side of the city is not good or evil. A Cubs fan is not different from a Red Sox fan. People who would rather push a

Ford car then drive a Chevy were not born that way. All human behavior could be explained with simple math using gaming theory, economic profit motive and cost benefit analysis. The most ardent fundamentalist Christian raised in a different country would be the most ardent fundamentalist Muslim burning churches and killing Christians. The most outspoken pro-American patriot fighting in Vietnam or Iraq if raised one of those 2 countries would be the most anti-American patriot killing every American he could. The old saying one sides terrorist is the other side's freedom fighter is very true.

     I watched the movie Independence Day when the earth was attacked by aliens who had superior technology and superior weapons and I thought everyone is making a hero of them and it's just like the people in the Middle East fighting the American army which has superior technology and superior weapons. The same story is played out in Star Wars a very popular movie franchise where the rebels are conducting guerrilla warfare against the very superior force. It all comes down to there is no good or evil no right side or wrong side. There is just my side and your side. There are two sides each of which wants to win.

     If person A values culture A so much that they will fight culture B who tries to destroy it. But if the people of culture A don't value culture A they will not fight very hard if culture B tries to destroy culture A. This is the situation we have in America and Europe today. For some reason, perhaps Cultural Marxism or a conspiracy or a fluke the last two generations of Western culture has trained and taught its children through forced public education that Western culture is bad, evil and of no value and not worth protecting or preserving. And because of this indoctrination the citizens of Western culture will not work very hard to defend it and save it from being destroyed. Western culture and society will be replaced by a culture that does value itself and has trained its citizens that their culture is good and worth preserving.

Remember people are not good or bad they are simply working to maximize their profit. A very honest man in a small town 200 years ago in America if put in America today might be a very dishonest man. In each case he is not good or evil, he is simply working to maximize his profit. 200 years ago, everyone in the town knew who he was and if he told a single lie he would never be able to do business again. But today in modern America he can sell used cars in the city of a million people and 2 years later moved to a new city with a million people and 2 years later moved to a different city with a million people and never see the same customer twice. Some people will say that in the first case the man 200 years ago he was a good honest man in the 2nd case today the man is a bad dishonest man. But, in each case the man is not good or evil, he is simply maximizing his profit. Doing what benefits him the most, acting in accordance with the environment he is in. People are not good or evil they are just trying to maximize their return on investment.

Mother Teresa feeding the poor is simply doing what makes her feel good. Mother Teresa gets more pleasure out of feeding the poor than she would snorting cocaine. A lion killing the previous male's cubs is acting in a selfish way. A lion sacrificing himself to save his cubs is acting in a selfish way. A person who goes to church and puts money in the collection plate every week so that he can get to heaven is acting in a selfish way. A person who pays his taxes and goes to work every day and buys a home and cuts the grass and washes his car and is good to his wife is acting in a selfish way. He is simply maximizing his profit. He is seeking pleasure and avoiding pain. He is seeking the carrot and avoiding the stick. There is not a single action in nature that is selfless. I used to offer my zoology students an A for the course if they could show me a single example in nature of a truly good, unselfish act and in 30 years I have not had a single example brought to my attention.

There have been many half thought out examples brought to my attention but on closer examination all are selfish. A male praying mantis who gets his head bitten off and eaten by the female he is mating with is giving her a nice protein snack before she lays his and her eggs. They now might have 300 healthy children. A male praying mantis who if he escaped before he was killed thus not giving her any protein that female might only produce 100 healthy eggs. So, the male who got his head bit off by the female is much more selfish. By sacrificing himself he produced three times the children of the one who did not. He beat the other male by 200 eggs. Every interaction by every individual whether it's a person at a soup kitchen, whether it's a rabbi, or priest, whether it's a teacher, whether it is a drug counselor or drug dealer, whether a policeman, whether it is a social worker. None of these people or their acts are good or evil they are simply done to maximize their own profit at that time. In fact, as I look at every interaction by every living organism on earth I come to the conclusion that there is no free will whatsoever. And if there is no free will at all how can any action be morally good or bad.

The environment dictates behavior. If you put a person in a society that only drives on the right side of the road then he will drive on the right side of the road. In America, a thief has a better strategy than a thief in a strict Muslim country that cuts the arm off a thief. How should a person live to maximize his profit? That depends on the environment, on their situation. The environment will shape behavior. If you put a man in a country where every girl only dates a boy who drives a car then every boy will try to get a car there is no free will in that. If you put a girl in a society where she will be rewarded for acting like a slut she will be a slut. If you put a girl in a society where she will be rewarded for acting like a prude she will act like a prude. Kim Kardashian in the environment of the United States behaves differently than the exact same Kim Kardashian in the environment of Saudi Arabia. The two hypothetical Kim Kardashians raised in two different environments are the exact same person, behaving in the exact same way. Even if that way is the exact opposite. There is no free will, in both of those cases she is not exercising any free will at all. But simply behaving as a chemical reaction a living organic robot. This robot simply behaves in the most profitable way possible. Each is acting in the most selfish way possible, maximizing the return on their investment. Maximizing their profit while minimizing their loss, avoiding the stick and seeking the carrot. And they do this in accordance with the environment they are in.

This is another problem people argue Nature vs Nurture while not understanding what they are saying or asking. Nurture is the environment a creature is in. You can always alter its environment and get a different behavior. Some fools would say see the environment has made the two hypothetical Kardashians act totally different, but that is not the case. They are acting the same, which is simply the way that will profit them the most. It just so happens in two different environments the most profitable actions might be different. This is no different than a person seeing a tiger at the zoo and running up to the cage or a person seeing a tiger in the jungle and running away from the Tiger. The actions while they might seem different on the surface are really the same. The person is doing what is safe and what profits them the most in each different environment.

As was said earlier people are neither bad nor good. And to think clearly and see the world clearly you must remove those designations. A doctor at the hospital who puts an antibiotic ointment on a patient's arm is good to the patient but evil to the bacteria. It is much clearer to say the patient is trying to profit at the expense of the bacteria and the bacteria are trying to profit at the expense of the patient. In the same way Organizations are neither bad nor good they simply work to maximize their profit. Every single interaction done by the smallest individual or the largest organization is simply to maximize their pleasure or profit. People are just seeking to get their carrot or what they conceived to be there carrot. Every interaction is selfish.

If we can understand that we can see that even the most innocent sounding branches of government are only there to serve themselves. Because remember there is no such thing as an unselfish act. When there is a child protection service from the government it is not there to protect children. There is no profit in that. They are there only to give lawyers jobs, give judges jobs, give social workers jobs, give government workers jobs etc. I personally knew a family that had a child with a major health issues that had to go through several surgeries. This child missed a great deal of school. The loving mother and father did everything they could to help this child and this loving family was attacked by child protection services and the school corporation. The social workers cogs in the giant government machine threatened and bullied this family repeatedly. After the family got the necessary paperwork and it was discovered that the series of surgeries had classified this child with now having a disability and was now a member of a governmentally protected group. The school and child protection services radically change their tune and were now very fearful of the family. It is important to note that in no way and at no time in this years-long battle was there any love or care showed for this child by of these government appointed people. Only her family and friends actually tried to help her.

No organization is there to help people, it is there to help the organization. This is a natural law that is never broken. Because any entity that does not help itself dies, goes extinct so does not exist for long to be seen. Some people may argue that even if the organization's primary purpose is to exist and help itself that it might as a byproduct of its actions also help children even if that isn't its primary goal. And some people seem to be content with this but I think these organizations even if some people argue that they do help a little overall they cause much more harm than good.

One example of this could be the divorce laws. Divorce in the United States is a money-making business. You have lawyer A representing party A another lawyer B representing party B and 3rd lawyer the judge who hears the trial. All these people make a living, a profit, get their carrot, make money, on this transaction. It pays these people to make this transaction as long complicated expensive and painful as possible. The people getting the divorce the mom the dad and the children do not benefit from this at

136

all. Many people see that this transaction is a losing game but they do not choose freely to go into this transaction. They have no choice. Each lawyer most often knows each other, they went to law school together, they play golf together, they belong to the same clubs. Each lawyer has knowledge of the family's finances so if they have 100,000 dollars in the bank it will be a 100,000-dollar divorce and if the family has 40,000 in the bank it will be a 40,000-dollar divorce. The lawyers have even changed the laws to help them make more money. Children are considered adults at 18 years old. and parents can tell them to go get a job and get out of the house. Unless the parents are divorced then the parents can be forced by government laws to pay for college until the kids are 23 years old. hundreds of thousands of dollars of more money is extracted from families this way. Even if the kids hate the parent and won't speak to them. This is done solely to make more business for the legal industry. In so many ways are people coerced by laws made of the lawyers, by the lawyers and for the lawyers to have job security laws are designed to ensure lawyers are needed. It is an interesting side note that now divorce has become so expensive such a danger and such a rigged system that many people are opting out and just avoiding marriage. The dangers are too great. Marriage is no longer profitable and the stick is too painful.

And it is not just the law profession although they have the added benefit of making the laws which other professions don't, the other professions must lobby and bribe and pay money to change laws but every profession does the same thing. It is the same with schools, the same with the medical industry, the same thing with the car industry. As soon as Tesla said I will sell cars directly to the public and bypass the dealerships the dealerships got together to fight for their survival, to fight for their profit. The same thing happened with Uber and Lift as soon people could get on a smart phone and have a ride waiting at the airport in 2 minutes or come home from a bar with 5 minutes notice at one third the cost of a regular taxi and 10 times the convenience the taxi companies and their many government officials gathered together to attack this new rival. It should be noted that is only with the government help that large and powerful corporations can so easily destroy smaller weaker corporations.

If a new wonderful technology came along to change the way we built houses the homebuilders Association would get together to fight that technology not to help homeowners but to help themselves. And they can only be successful in stopping this new help with a large and powerful government. If there was a great medicine that was invented that made doctors obsolete the American Medical Association would fight it. Not to help people be healthy but to help protect their profit. Evidence for this is apparent in that one of the simplest economic theories of supply and demand America has had a shortage of doctors for 50 years. 50 years ago, a hypothetical American king could have said I decree my people need more doctors every medical school will double the number of doctors as quickly as possible. Medical schools will crank out more doctors, we must increase production of doctors. In simple supply and demand it would then lower the cost of medical care. But, the AMA the American Medical Association and all the associated networks of doctors and healthcare providers know that solution is not in their best interest. This is just one stunning example among hundreds of stunning examples which show every act by every organization is an act of and from complete selfishness. Any help done by a group to another group outside of themselves is purely accidental and coincidental.

Things that seem to be exceptions to the rule can be when thinks along the lines of brainwashing have taken place. In these cases, like the Stockholm syndrome a group can be taught to hate themselves to such an extent that the self-loathing group will voluntarily harm itself to the benefit of another group but this is extremely rare and short lived as this mental disorder leads to its own extinction. Imagine if all the laws could be downloaded into a very intelligent computer and laws could then be distributed fairly and impartially by this electronic legal system doing away with the need of lawyers and judges. The entire Bar Association of America would be up in arms fighting this. Not because they want people to have fair and just law or easy access to the law or inexpensive laws but because it would threaten their profit.

Chapter 18
Instinct for self-preservation

Someone once said that the nearest thing to immortality is a temporary government program. Once a government program is established there is a huge investment in getting it started, getting it going, maintaining it, funding for it. The program has so much inertia, so much mass, so much investment, that once it is going no one profiting from it wants to stop it. It is important to remember nothing disappears of its own accord. No sane vigorous growing thing commits suicide and ends its own existence. No organism, no agency, no entity, gives up its own life. Suicide is rare, most things individuals, tribes, clans, businesses, governments etc. don't consciously commit suicide. The budgets of these government programs just get bigger and bigger every year. Now this should be a red flag i.e. a warning to people. If the program was working shouldn't it be solving the problem not making it worse. Every government help program if it did work should put itself out of business. For example, welfare programs should educate people so they are not on welfare after a couple years and then welfare should be gone. There would be no need for it. This is the difference between feeding a man a fish and teaching him how to fish for himself. All drug rehabilitation programs, education programs, job programs, school lunch programs, think about this any that worked, if they did work, they would solve the problem and put themselves out of business. But that doesn't happen

I cannot think of a single example of the American government setting up a program that worked so well it was declared a great success and removed because it was so successful. Has any

Government program ever accomplished its goal and fulfilled its mission. The lack of success for any government program ever might seem strange, until you remember gaming theory and profit motive and follow the money. It does no good for the head of the welfare agency and all his highly-paid administrators to work themselves out of a job. That is not their goal. Their goal like everything living is to grow, expand, increase.

The only example I can think of when a worker did his job and worked himself out of the job is the Irish wolfhound. They were so effective at killing wolves that the last wolf went extinct in Ireland around 1700 and then soon the big dogs went extinct. The Irish Wolfhound we see today in dog shows is only a recreation. But the dogs were probably not smart enough to see the profit motive and the loyal dogs worked themselves out of a job and paid the price with their lives This is a mistake and sacrifice no intelligent calculating smiling human politician would ever do. Everyone who really did their job should be getting closer and closer to putting himself or herself out of business. Welfare agencies profit the most i.e. benefit the most by keeping welfare going and growing making it bigger and bigger every year as big as possible. This is done by any agency that must spend all the money it gets in a year or lose it and try to get more next year

One of the best illustrations of this is unneeded company meetings. The incessant need to have meetings and to fill up all the meeting time. Often this is simply done because part of a person's job is to schedule and facilitate meetings and if they were very efficient and did their job well there would be no need of the meeting or it could be cut shorter. This is very like the case of professional development. I would wager that if a company, corporation, school, or any organization had its professional development budget cut in half and its number of meetings or meeting times cut in have overall efficiency and productivity would not be reduced.

I have a friend in the military, a thinking man who after many years in the Military and close to retirement has come up a unifying principle which rules the military he called his personal theory. "The Theory of Relevancy." He told me that this was the driving force behind military policy. He explained that every program, everything, every boot, gun, boat, plane, tank, truck, job, rank, assignment, division, branch, spent a great deal of energy just to prove they were relevant. He was quite a history buff and explained that the Marines were almost done away with but during the Korean War proved their relevancy, and continued to spend energy to do so. Tasks done by army, navy, or marines were a batter of who was relevant. Every promoted person had to justify his promotion and prove his relevancy. Every new assignment the person had to come in and show why he was needed so much. Even if the best thing overall for the military and the American people would have been for him to say. Hey, this job is really not needed but he couldn't do that. He had to prove he was relevant. He said one of the plainest examples of this was the US invasion of Grenada. Every branch and everyone in every branch wanted to be relevant. According to his guy the marines could have done the whole mission with zero causalities. But because the Army and air force and navy had to all have a part and each wanted the biggest most important most relevant part they all got in each other's way and complicated things and got 19 men unnecessarily killed. Four Navy SEALs drowned at the start of a pre-invasion reconnaissance mission after an air drop from an Air Force transport plane. The Army combat units couldn't talk to Navy support ships because their radios weren't compatible. Navy people objected to refueling Army helicopters. Marine people didn't want to fly Army Rangers into battles on Marine helicopters. Apparently, it was a big mess made into a bigger mess by everyone wanting to be relevant.

I listened to him for a while he had spent a great deal of time putting together this "Theory of Relevancy" and I thought that is just another set of words, a good memorable set of words, to describe the selfish instinct for self-preservation. People must justify their jobs and if you look at what anyone in an organization is doing through the lens of how are they trying to justify their job or how are they trying to prove their relevance it will result in some clear seeing and thinking. No one wants to commit suicide either literally or professionally.

The instinct for self-preservation is apparent in every interaction in the animal kingdom, and the human business world, and the human government world. Whenever creatures interact they always act in such a way to preserve themselves if they don't then they will go extinct and won't be around to not act in a way to cause self-preservation. I've used the example of government programs which always preserve themselves but the same is also true of individuals or groups or any organization. The buggy whip company and all the people dependent on buggy whips worked very hard to preserve themselves. The typewriter industry worked very hard to preserve itself. Blockbuster video worked very hard to preserve itself. They were simply unable to given the changing environment.

This is one fascinating thing about Western civilization it is the sole example that I can think of where the dominant in power, majority civilization and population voluntarily agreed to become the subordinate, out of power, minority civilization and population. However, this does not overturn gaming theory, or profit motive. It is simply that in chasing the carrot and avoiding the stick two generations of Western society have been trained, and educated that the mere presence of their society causes them pain. So, they avoid the pain and seek the pleasure and they have been indoctrinated to find pleasure in the destruction of their society. They have been brainwashed to find self-preservation painful and self-destruction pleasurable.

Chapter 19
Know What is Invested

This chapter could have been entitled appreciate what they have invested. When people have an investment in anything, an idea, a concept or a political party it costs them to change that idea. It cost them a great deal of pain to admit they have been wrong and given their energy and resources to something that they shouldn't have. Almost no one can bear the pain of that admission. So, you must know what people have invested when you try to reason with them.

A person who has been a Democrat their entire life who now has evidence that it's better to be a Libertarian must first face a great deal of pain, admit they were wrong. This pain of admitting you have been a fool is a huge stick and remember from the previous chapter a stick and a carrot are all we have. Nothing else will control human behavior. In order to avoid the stick, the punishment, the pain, sometimes it's just easier if you've been wrong to just keep on being wrong. This is especially true if there's really no punishment to being wrong. This is one of the biggest problems in modern society. No one dies for being wrong and stupid anymore.

If I think I can breathe underwater If I have the opinion and you must respect my opinion that I can breathe under water and I jump in the ocean and try to breathe, I will die. I have a great deal of punishment for being wrong. If I think I can drink poison and I do and I die. I would get a great deal of punishment for being wrong. If I think the gun is unloaded and I really left a bullet in the gun and I pulled the trigger and shoot someone or myself I have a great deal of punishment from being wrong. It would cost me a great deal, it is very painful to be wrong in some situations. However, in political discussion and ideas unless you are the leader of a country it really doesn't cost you anything to be wrong.

In modern society being wrong really doesn't end your life. In fact, we have a new term for correctness it's called politically correct. Which of course almost by definition means it's different than just being correct. If you are not politically correct it could cost you friendships, dating opportunities, access to social events, job opportunities. So once someone has invested in an idea, a political platform, a political viewpoint, a political party, etc. it is very painful for them to change but it is not very painful for them to be wrong, to keep doing it the wrong way. In the natural world if you think a poisonous snake is not poisonous or you think Lions eat plants or you think the bear won't eat your children it costs you. But holding the wrong political viewpoint costs you nothing.

You can be absolutely wrong in your political opinion and nothing happens to you. You can think paying people to not work will make them work, whatever. You pay zero consequences. So, in this regard you can see that once people have done something a certain way for a long time it is almost impossible to get them to change, and, why should they? There is no punishment for being wrong and there's quite a bit of punishment and pain for admitting you have been wrong. In politically correct America there is no profit in correcting a mistake. In order to understand how governments, work and how they are supported to you must first understand and learn to appreciate what people have already invested in their ideas so far.

To understand political loyalties, you must understand this cost of political investment This is sometimes called the gambler's dilemma, not to be confused with the prisoner's dilemma. It is also taught in every college freshman psychology class it can best be summed up as; people can't accept the fact that they have been wrong. They don't know when to cut their loses, and admit they've been wrong. It seems impossible for some people to do this. This is again because it is unprofitable to do so or expense. They have too much invested in being right. A woman who has been a socialist for 30 years can't just say I have been wrong all my life, all my work and effort and energy have been a waste and a lose I was a loser. That is too expensive to throw all that away. Better to just go on deluding themselves it is easier, cheaper less expensive than facing the truth. A person will stay in a poker game until they lose everything because they can't quit after having lost twenty bucks and say I've been had or I've been wrong.

There is an old story, which illustrates the point of this lesson well it is about an old gold prospector who came into town one day to get supplies. He lived worse than an animal and was searching for gold. He knew he was near finding the mother lode and all his hard work would pay off. Many people in the town thought the old man was crazy there is no gold in this area anymore, all the claims had been mined out and no new ones had been found by the best methods. The old man had devoted the last forty years of his life to hitting the mother lode, the jackpot. The old man came to the general store about once every three months when his supplies ran out. He bought the supplies from the storeowner on credit saying I will pay you back ten times when I strike it rich. I asked the store owner if he ever expected to get paid back by the old man. He just shook his head no. There ain't no gold out there. I then asked the storeowner why he didn't tell the old miner that there was no gold out there. The store owner said oh that old man knows there is no gold out there. He knows this county better than you and I put together, but he can't stop looking. This left me more confused so I said why if the old man knew there was no gold out there why did he keep looking why couldn't he stop. The storeowner looked at me smiled sadly and said because: If he was to ever give up and quit looking for gold he would first have to admit that the last forty years of his life have been a waste! And he can't do that, no one could, it would kill him. His knees ache every day from standing in cold steams working a gold pan. He back hurts from being bent over all the time. Arthritis hurts his whole body as he sleeps on the cold hard ground in a bed roll. He never married, never had children, when he dies no one will miss him. No one can admit that they have been that wrong for that long. To do so would kill him. So, he keeps going out to search of gold that isn't there.

There is a similar story which illustrates the same point about a man digging for gold with his bare hands. His fingers sore and bleeding his fingernails broken and dirty he has done it this way for years. Someone hands him a shovel instead of being grateful he breaks the shovel over their head and goes back to doing things the old way. How many times have we heard "we have always done it this way" Las Vegas picks clean victim after victim from this same well understood principle. People stay in a bad job for twenty years just because you have already stayed in it for ten years. Don't stay in an abusive marriage for thirty years just because you have already endured ten years. So, what you were a fool for ten years its better than being a fool for twenty years but most people can't admit they have been wrong because they have too much invested in something it might be a time investment, money investment, or an emotional investment.

This investment principle can affect every aspect of a person's life. I have a friend who is a very intelligent successful man and he drives a big heavy clumsy gas guzzling van to work every day because he has a trailer that he might pull because he bought a boat and needed the trailer to pull the boat with the van. Trailer and boat both have sat beside his garage for six years. He can't admit that he should not have ever bought the trailer and it was a mistake and he can't sell the boat at a loss to get rid of it that would be a mistake and who can admit one of those? So, he sets a boat beside his garage on a trailer and drives a big van he hates every day to work because of this principle he has an investment in that boat, an emotional investment but it grows bigger every year. Next year he will still have the van because he will be even less likely to sell it because his investment will be even bigger next year. This illustrates why seeming illogical behavior is logical, and why people do the things they do.

To summarize this chapter, you must realize that the only things that control human behavior is the carrot and stick. Someone admitting they been wrong and self-humiliating themselves and facing themselves and admitting their own stupidity is so much punishment that people avoid it at all costs. It is the ultimate stick one of the ultimate punishments incredibly painful and people will seek to avoid at all costs.

There is an old saying which is true. It is easier to fool a person than for a person to admit he has been fooled. It costs you a great deal of pain to admit you have been fooled so once people have investment in government running a certain way it has a great deal of inertia and will keep running that way and who is going to admit they have been supporting a bad idea and inflict that much and pain and suffering upon themselves who is going to hit themselves with that big stick just for the sake of some truth that really doesn't benefit them anyway. It's not like they went from believing cobras were not poisonous to believing cobra are poisonous. Which is a life or death truth. You die if you don't get it right. However, in modern society we don't have that many life or death truths. Good parasites don't kill their hosts.

Chapter 20
No good leaders anymore.

Why aren't there any good leaders anymore. Well if you've read the book so far you know the answer to that question. There's no benefit, no profit to being a good leader today. If you remember from a previous chapter there was great profit to be a good pirate leader, the pirate captain. If you are not a good leader of the pirate ship you didn't get any pay. But a modern CEO, a modern business leader, a modern boss gets paid regardless of how good a job he does. Add to this the fact that there is no punishment, no stick to being a bad leader today. Many problems of organizations have difficult and painful solutions if someone came into a school system and said we have lazy students who are not working, we have ignorant teachers who really don't know the material, we have parents who don't make sure their kids do the homework, our students are the kids of all the Walmart videos you see on YouTube. They would never get the job. A potential leader by telling the truth will cause no one to hire him. So, the leader who lives and offers an easy solution even if it is a false solution to a problem will be hired over one who is smarter, more honest and can solve the problems.

The same is true for a politician. A politician who tells the truth will never be elected. The CEO of a company who says this industry is disappearing and we are going to have to make some drastic painful changes and we will probably not pay the stock dividends we have in the past will not be hired. The consultant who looks at a company and says I can turn this problem around in six months I offer you this magic bullet that will fix everything easily and painlessly will be hired. Now this consultant will be on to a new consulting job in six months or a year and so they really don't have anything to lose by not solving the problem.

This is especially true of government grants almost all grants run out in two or three years almost all the problems they are supposed to solve take many years to solve. The person who offers the solution is already paid and gone by the time the solution never happens. By the time everyone sees that the problem was never solved that person is long gone and been paid off and is onto another consulting gig.

This stands in stark contrast to what we used to see in the past when the leader of an organization's performance directly tied into that person's reward. In the ancient world, a leader of hunters for the tribe who did not find the mammoth or make the kill or the leader of a pirate ship that did not find plunder or the trail boss of a cow herd he did not get their cattle to market all those men suffered because they were poor leaders. A band of ancient warriors who had a poor leader would kill him. A group of employees in the modern age who have a poor leader can do nothing about it and usually just must wait until their poor leader is promoted or moves on to a new job. And perhaps their new leader is no better, but they can do nothing about it. From politics, to car companies, to schools, to police departments, to government agencies, in the modern world all of them reward bad leadership and punish good leadership so according to the theme of this book we should get more bad leadership. And I think that is what we have seen in the last 50 years.

Another point is that many problems have expensive solutions, difficult solutions, boring solutions, and unpalatable solutions. The president, executive, principle, board director, leader who says we are in bad shape and there is no easy solution to this. it's going to take a lot of hard work to fix and it will not solve the problem to everyone's satisfaction. He is not saying anything people want to hear. People don't want to hear that there is no magic solution. Who is going to buy that? So that person will not sell his idea and no one will pay to hear him. But bosses who aren't going to be around in the long term anyway will call on the charlatan who preaches easy solutions or lies. They only need to look good for a 2-3-year plan and then move on so they would rather give the illusion of solving problems then actually get bogged down in an ugly difficult mess with tough solutions. This aspect of understanding behavior is to ask the question "who profits from this". This is one reason why the pie in the sky dreamer will and can get away with believing he has a better way than reality. This is not a deadly mission which requires reality.

It is also true of most executive positions, very few bosses in modern American society are in a position of power by earning respect and trust of their subordinates. In fact, we have the insane situation where most workers be they teachers, nurses, technicians, lab Tec's, factory workers, policeman, fireman, etc. who have worked in a place have seen 3-4 bosses come and go. They have actually been there, at their place of work, doing their job longer, understanding their job better, then the boss they are working for has. How can this be? The boss is simply building his resume and moving on to the next job and never stays or intends to stay anywhere more than three years. I used to think that was illogical until I applied gaming theory, profit motive and other principles of this book to the situation.

In the modern world, a leader benefits most to move to a higher paying job every chance he gets. With no concern for the company. It is profitable to not stay anywhere more than 3 years because you can't be blamed for anything. And since you are not going to be here in 3 years why stir up trouble and do anything for the long-term good. It is better to just do showy, glitzy things that look good but have no real substance because those kinds of things will profit you the most. Even the colleges and universities have gotten into the act. Whenever possible they have lobbied senator's legislatures to require more education of administrative personal. A certain degree or certificate is required to do a particular job. Not because you really couldn't do the job without it but because it eliminates competition, and stops free enterprise and forces people to pay large sums of money to universities to get good jobs.

Formal Education has stopped being a doorway to a better life but now it is a roadblock. It's not that education allows you to get a job, it's that lack of a degree keeps you from getting a job. The universities even advertise this fact. They run ads that show a person saying something like "I wish I could get the promotion or a better paying job but I lack the degree". Many have even dropped the pretext of you need training to do a better job. It's simple you need the degree to unlock doors and get over barriers not for education. In fact, this has like so many complications made the situation worse. It used to be that the best worker became the foreman and the best teacher the department head and the best department head became the principle. But now a different degree is needed for each position so the natural order of the best rising to the top has been disrupted. And the universities are simple doing what

154

profits them. Just follow the money. With the internet, everything is available all the university lectures all the math, science, all knowledge all education is free and available for anyone who wants it. But the universities control who gets the piece of paper. I look forward to the day that all the universities go the way of block buster and the buggy whip companies and we have a world class education for free for everyone which is possible with the internet.

Why are there no good leaders anymore?

1. Organizations, and governments don't attract the best people. A person who wants to live from the labor of others is exactly the opposite kind of person that you would want to lead you.
2. Also no one who tells the truth can be elected to government so the process not only attracts criminals and users only liars and deceivers can successfully become leaders in government today.
3. Modern leaders have no skin in the game. A politician can break every campaign promise he made, get money from lobbying interests and change his mind on every issue. They can close factories that hurt his constituents and none of this harms him. It is a far day from when a Pleistocene leader of a hunting band made bad decisions which caused the hunt to fail and he also starved.
4. Followers don't get to pick their leaders, so the best leaders, the smartest, the best strategists don't rise to a position of leadership. This is true in every organization. Every school, has a principal dumber and less capable than the smartest teacher. Every post office has a postal worker smarter and more capable than the supervisor. Every factory has a foreman dumber and less capable than his smartest

worker. Every company as an executive dumber and less capable than the smartest worker underneath him. Every police chief is dumber and less capable than his smartest and most capable officer. Every politician, president, governor, senator, Congressman had many constituents who they ruled over who were much smarter and more capable than they are.

This is a modern situation and one that is relatively recent. For most of human history. The leader of the tribe, the captain of the pirate ship, the chieftain of the clan, the foreman of the line, the lead hunter, was the smartest and most capable member of that group and of course was PART of that group.

CHAPTER 21
Why Big Government can't work.
Communism Socialism and Utopias don't work never have worked and can't work.

Communism has failed every single time it has been attempted. Communes have failed every single time they have been tried. Utopias have failed every time they have been started. It is a perfect record of destruction. It seems like in every political discussion the left wing, the socialists, the communists the SJW's have they always come back to the same answer "If we could all just be communists" "if we could all just be more socialist" "if we could all just cooperate then we would have a great government". If we could just do communist right. But as can be seen basically these communists, these socialists, these big government liberals just want everyone to pool their resources together and share and cooperate. If everyone would just be nice and share then everyone would be nicer. This of course means nothing. They seem to skip the step that if everyone would just be nice then we would not need government at all.

They make the illogic leap of, no one is nice so we need a big government to make everyone nice. Not seeming to understand that if people are not nice and people are selfish then giving huge amount of power to a few people will result in them not being very nice but now with a huge amount of power not to be nice with. That is no solution because as has been shown in the previous chapters those are the type of organizations and rules and regulations that reward cheating the most and the people that seek those positions of power are the ones most likely to abuse it.

The idea that everyone can just not cheat and will work for the interest of the collective like they were insects such as termites and ants is an interesting concept. It is often thought of as noble and sometimes attempted by utopian society people. Communists have tried it. Liberals have tried it. Socialists have tried it. Many people don't understand why it has never worked it the past and will not work in the future. It simply doesn't work and can never work. It does not survive and never will survive. It cannot survive simple because it is unstable and mathematically unsound. It is unstable because it is vulnerable to cheating. Any situation that is vulnerable to cheating will experience cheating any situation or government that provides a resource will have that resource exploited. It is unstable and won't work in the real world. These are simple economic principles.

The examples are endless. You can think of several on your own. For example: vampire bats will share blood after a night of feeding. The bat is not being kind or generous. A bat that has not gotten any blood can beg its neighbor who will regurgitate some blood up and share. They do this because it is profitable to do so. A bat that shares some of its blood is not really harmed but a bat that did not feed that night and can't find anyone who will share with it will likely die. So, buying the insurance is worth the price. According to vampire bat physiology, evolution and the parameters of this planet sharing is a profitable behavior for vampire bats. There is no good, evil, selfish or generous there is simply a system set up so that sharing is profitable to these bats, at this time, in this environment. One could easily imagine an environmental change in which food grew scarcer and meals so far apart that sharing was now a detriment. The established behavior of sharing would no longer be profitable and the odd individuals who didn't share would be rewarded. After a while this new behavior would become established. Each society's behavior is in a constant state of flux always moving toward maximum profit. A model of this changing behavior could be set up by a gaming theory modeler he could setup something like this. If you don't eat, and no one will share with you, it costs you 10 points. If you have eaten and you share with someone else, it only costs you 2 points. So, it is not a costly thing to share for a vampire bat, but a very expensive thing to not share. In fact, by the values we set you could share 5 times before it cost you 10 points. Any bat that did not share would not be shared with and would die. The dead bat would not send his selfish behavior into the next generation. It is good insurance to keep on good terms with your neighbors, if you are a vampire bat. Gaming theory and profit motive rule our interactions. You could always change the values and assume it cost more to share than be selfish and guess what? the selfish trait would increase. Because every action done by an individual that is not selfish will lead to its extinction.

This is something that liberals don't seem to understand. I had a friend who taught Humanities and he explained this great theoretical system of society called social three folding. In this system society is broken up into 3 parts the political, cultural and economic and each part should be separate and not have influence in the others. For example, religion is a cultural thing and should not be mixed with politics nor should it be mixed with the financial or economic. Another example is economic things like money should not influence political things or put pressure on religion or culture. I said ok that is a good idea but what do you do when a business in the economic sphere tries to bribe a person in political power to change laws to favor the business. He said you don't allow that to happen each sphere must be separate. I said how do you keep people from cheating and using influence to get what they want. He said the three parts stay separate. I said how can you keep them separate when all anyone has to do is flash some money and people will be tempted to take it. He said in social three folding people are not allowed to take bribes. I said they aren't now. He said laws that allow lobbing are legalized bribery and I said yes but there is plenty of illegal bribery also and how would this make that disappear. He said it's not part of social three folding. I realized that he was too stupid to talk to anymore but did tell him that any system of government that was vulnerable to cheating was unstable and this fantasy government where everyone stayed in their own little sandbox and never tried to get what they wanted by any means was just as effective as a warden at a maximum-security prison saying everyone just play nice and expecting it to happen. I'm sure him being an intellectual just assumed I was too simple minded to understand the complexities of social three folding. I think he was just an academic who didn't live in the real world and had a protected career in academy so he protected his fantasy world. It is interesting that I have had many conversations with degreed, liberal, intellectuals who could not get a job or even support themselves outside of the University system talk is this way so out of reality.

Another example, which illustrates why most types of social engineering won't work, is something everyone has seen, a field of weeds. If a communist leader with a manifesto could just convince all the weeds to just grow one foot tall and stop, then all the weeds would get the same amount of sunlight as if they all grew 10 feet tall. But they could save all the cost of growing so tall, the expense of deeper roots, thicker stalks, the material used to build great height could be saved just think of the advantages. The plants would also be safer avoiding the risk of being blown over in the wind. It seems if the in the world of weeds if they could just cooperate they could all have such a much better life. However, a smart person now realizes that is not realistic. The reason such a theoretically wonderful better system will not work is because such an arrangement is vulnerable to cheating, therefore it is unrealistic. Any plant that cheated and grew beyond the others would be rewarded, by getting more sunlight. Cheating would be profitable cheating would be rewarded, any behavior that is rewarded will be increased. Consequently, this scenario cannot last because it is unrealistic. Instead, what we have is reality, all weeds trying to outdo each other. They grow to the maximum height they can obtain to defeat the others while factoring in other considerations involved in the cost of height. Such as the vulnerability to wind, obviously, any plant that grew so tall that the wind tipped it over would not be acting in its own best profit. Obviously, any plant that grew very short would not be in its own best interest. The cost in materials must be weighed against the benefit of more sunlight, and danger of tipping over. This is what we see any time that we look at a field all cheating; it is stable, it is fair, it is beautiful. Do you understand if everyone in the system is cheating it is fair, but if only half the people in a system are cheating it is unfair? If everyone is openly selfish then no one is being selfish.

How quickly can society react to the changes. Remember a committee like a senate committee or government committee cannot react quickly. So, if the worlds resources become in short supply, food becomes rare, fresh water a luxury, criminal activity controlled by the government instead of citizens. Then America will not be able to cope with a change in the environment the people of America will suffer greatly until it becomes so bad that the government goes extinct. This might change into a fascist type of martial law which would probably still reward parasites and cheaters and protect criminals because it would be very vulnerable to cheating. A friend of the soldier would get extra food while a man who didn't appreciate the soldiers might have his daughters raped. Now if this fascist government didn't give the soldier a gun and take away the citizens gun the father or daughter might not get raped or abused.

I am still amazed at the people who say but if you didn't have the soldiers everyone would start raping the girls. This ignores the obvious fact that if soldiers had not been given guns and the people disarmed the citizens could not have been victimized and the girl would be armed as well as the soldiers. Perhaps one of the best things to happen for the people of America would be a quick, complete collapse of the dollar and government power so that people could just start governing themselves. I don't think people are so evil that they would cut loose like lunatic released out of an asylum. People would start to do what would benefit them the most. Anything that profits them and helps them to live. Eat, grow reproduce, raise a family. And in a society where everyone can defend themselves and everyone is allowed and encouraged to defend themselves being an "evil victimizer is not profitable. A rapist would likely be killed by his victim, if not the first time then the second or third. Every rape would carry a risk of death. Rape robber, assault would become expensive and dangerous, every act being a risk of death. It is interesting that in modern America much work, time effort and money is invested so that the criminal can commit his crimes in safety. A cheater of the system or criminal can do his crimes with almost no risk of death. Modern American government has made these things safe and profitable and attractive. One of my favorite quotes from Malcolm X is "it is criminal to teach a man not to defend himself in a hostile world". The reality of the situation is. It is profitable to the government to not allow citizens to defend themselves. It is profitable for government to take away the rights and abilities of citizens to defend themselves and then charge them for that service.

Big government just can't react fast enough to stay ahead of the exploiters and advantage takers. Suppose a government program that takes a couple of years to go through congress is passed and becomes policy. Now as soon as it hits the street any selfish individuals can start to think of ways to take advantage of the system, to cheat and profit by it. Their response is immediate, a matter of days but suppose the government wants to fix the problem close the loophole it in response takes years to get laws passed so the loophole is open to be exploited for years. Finally, the loophole gets closed after years of abuse. Then the next day individual people can figure ways around it. This is like a giant slow-moving train trying to keep up with a sports car. The government simply cannot respond quickly enough to close loophole to cheaters it's too big it has too much inertia.

This is one reason a government cannot do a giveaway program correctly. There is no way to just do communism right. Bigger government can never work because of its size, it is too big and too slow in response time to keep up with cheats. But lest anyone think I am only picking on government give away programs one prime example is the SUV vehicles. In 1979, the government decided all cars should get better gas mileage and put café regulations on all cars. Well the car manufactures now sell trucks called SUVs that are exempt from fuel mileage requirement to people and the loophole might get closed by 2010 so a 30-year lag time which is typical of government response time. Imagine that a government mandate for all cars to get better fuel mileage and this takes years to get through congress and the next day after it becomes law. Ford, Chevy and Chrysler just start pushing pickup trucks on the buying public. Motor companies advertise how cool the trucks and sport utilities vehicles are. The CEOs of those companies already knew the law was coming. They probably have donated money to the politicians and are friends and comrades anyway. And so, all the good supposed to be done by the CAFÉ standards which took years to put in place and costs millions of dollars to accomplish can be circumvented in about a week.

Another example of a seeming illogical waste of resources that illustrates the point that any theoretical pay out in any society is not the same as the actual payout. A correct theoretical payout is possible to model it only requires people and scientists to measure all the inputs in a system this is one area Karl Marx with his very simplistic childlike innocence missed. Look at an entire order of animals who have spent millions of years evolving the most economically profitable way to live the deer family. Male deer spend enormous sums of energy growing huge antlers to fight each other during the mating season. After the mating season, they drop off because they are so heavy and burdensome. Deer antlers are the fastest growing bone in the animal kingdom, the males must

164

eat a great deal of nutrient rich food the results of which are shed off as soon as they can all that work just thrown on the ground and wasted. The same food that could go to the females. The minerals in that food could be used to help grow the skeleton of a fetus but instead are taken by males to grow antlers bigger than other males that are otherwise useless and will only be shed. This whole growing antlers, taking nutrients from mothers and babies for all the calcium to end up on the ground seems to be a very wasteful arms race. So, the best optimum strategy for all deer if every deer would cooperate and not cheat, in an idealized communistic or socialist deer society, with maximize overall success. The most good for all would be for all the males to grow no antlers at all or at least very small ones. Now, with all the savings in energy and other resources the female deer could eat all the good nutrient rich food. Every deer's offspring could have a better, healthier start in life. This is somewhat like prenatal health care. However, such a system is again unstable because it is vulnerable to being taken advantage of. If it did exist, any male that cheated and grew bigger antlers than the agreed upon size limit would be more successful in collecting females. He would mate with more females, leaving more offspring. The cheating trait behavior would spread. Anyone who followed the rules would be penalized at the cost of fewer offspring and this rule following cooperative trait would be punished and would die out.

For these reasons, it is obvious why there is no utopian society, even after millions of attempts and thousands of years of trying. There is never been one successful commune or utopian society all have been dismal failures. No one can create a utopian society because anyone trying to create that society who believes that society is possible ignores the well know repeatedly proven factor of cheaters. A society that does not take into account, that does not consider the cheaters is unstable precisely because it is vulnerable to cheating. The best that humanity can do is figure out what things it feels are important, what it wants to promote and then get as close to the theoretical ideal as possible with no profit for cheating. The government of a Pirate ship is about as close to Utopia as one can get in the real world. One obvious example of a society that does not take this into account is modern American society. The American Government subsidizes and promotes what seem to be on the surface seemingly undesirable traits like irresponsibility, helplessness, victim-hood, stupidity, dependence, cowardice and liar's cheaters and criminals. These behaviors are prospering like a well-tended garden given extra water fertilizer sunshine and care. Every well baby program, teen pregnancy program, victim's advocacy group, and welfare group not only encourages these traits but increases these traits. Of course, as these traits increase so does the need for more government so government has grown itself which is the purpose of everything. The stated purpose of these programs was to make them unnecessary but as anyone can see that does not and will not happen, but the programs spreads the very problem it is supposed to solve. Therefore, the national war on poverty has increased poverty. It has made poverty profitable. Free apartments, free medical care and free food stamps, free books, free heat, free cell phones, free internet access. Every time a government program is put in place to fix a problem it grows the problem. Because that problem has now been made profitable to have is profitable for people to have the problem is profitable for government workers to deal with this problem is profitable for companies to provide products to deal with this problem. As can be seen anything that becomes profitable will increase, no just follow the money. And big government is big business.

As a final note, I would like to address the argument I hear repeatedly and again from well-meaning leftists who believe the government is answerable to the people and so government cannot abuse the people. They hold this party line in spite of the fact that numerous governments have abused their people. The greatest murderers, mass killings genocides and abuses have all been governments. It seems that many leftists believe corporations are evil. Corporations will conspire to act selfishly for their own benefit. That corporations will exploit people and gather resources for their benefit but that governments will not. I have explained to these people that the government is just a super corporation. Everything that leftists fear from corporations, the government which is just a super corporation can do to them much more strongly. When I point this out I am always answered with but the government should be accountable to the people or I hear that people vote in the government as if people control the government. I have explained that this is ludicrous. Corporations are much more answerable to the people than the government is. A simple boycott of Chick-fil-A can cause its business to disintegrate. A simple boycott of Ford Motor Company for one month will destroy that company, a simple boycott of United Airlines will destroy that company. But no one can boycott the United States government. Everyone knows if a corporation is allowed to become a monopoly and has no competition it becomes too powerful and can abuse people. But the government is the biggest monopoly. You may get to vote for president every four years. But that is not even a remedy. There is only a choice between the Democrats anointed candidate or the Republicans anointed candidate. In American government, there is no choice of who is president. You only get to select from the lesser of two evils and that is all. (I like the phrase the lesser of two evils is really the evil of two lessers) And you only get to do it once every four years not with your instant purchasing power on a daily basis. There is no way for American public dissatisfied with its government to vote in changes. It is a thousand times easier for a disgusted American public to alter the course of a single business or even a huge corporation than it is for a disgusted American public to change its government. This is another reason why big government communism and socialism does not work. And does not represent the people for anyone to make the argument that corporations does not work in the best interest of people but big governments does is a lapse of logic.

Chapter 22
Carrot or Stick

All there is. All there has ever been. And the only thing there is. To control any population, organization, tribe, clan, gang, etc. is the stick or the carrot. In the previous chapter I explained this as profit motive. Which is exactly the same thing as carrot and stick, reward and punishment. In simple terms, the pain or the pleasure. People seek pleasure and avoid pain. They seek the carrot and avoid the stick. They seek profit and avoid loss. That is all there is. Now this may seem depressing but once we realize that all there is, is a carrot or a stick reward or punishment then honest progress can be made. We could have societies where everyone plays by the rules but why don't we? If you read the book so far you realize it must be because there is some profit to be had in cheating there is some profit to be made by not playing by the rules. It must be someone is benefiting from the current situation and is continuing to perpetuate that situation. It all depends on how you set the game up It turns out that cheating is not profitable in all conditions only in certain artificial conditions. For example, only if the government subsidizes cheating will cheating occur. It is an illusion to believe that respect will exist as a virtue or (call it a trait to be objective) if there is no profit in it. Now a simple slap in the face for disrespect will make it unprofitable to be disrespectful. But the police arrest a man for slapping another man in the face who is disrespectful then they're no longer is any punishment for being disrespectful there's only punishment for stopping disrespect. If you want it to be a benefit for respectful behavior then respectful behavior must be rewarded. You must have some combination of both profit and cost, reward and punishment, carrot and stick applied to make respect a common trait. This answers another question of why people are so rude to each other in modern American society. The answer is simple. People have no benefit, no profit, no reward for being polite, in days of yore a man who was rude to another got punched in the nose. But now that is assault and the judges and lawyers and court personal circle like vultures to try the cases. So, you can say about anything to anyone and the risk is low of having a negative consequence. So now we have rude behavior common. The days when a man's word was his bond only happened because if you ever broke your word, no one would ever deal with you again, you might get challenged to a duel and be killed. It was very unprofitable. It was profitable to keep your word. Good people are not good they are seeking profit. Things are all directed by the outlined principles.

So, once we have established that all there is to control behavior is the carrot and the stick we must decide what behavior we want to encourage and reward with the carrot and decide what behavior we want to discourage and punish with the stick. If we do this clearly and logically we will have a society that behaves in the manner the game is set up. That is in a manner that maximizes each individual's profit. This was very clear from the previous chapter where I laid out the articles of piracy you can see that there are very clear carrots and very clear sticks. The sticks are very severe in the carrots are very tangible. That is the case of a very efficient organization. An organizational where no one can tell exactly what the sticks are nor exactly what the carrots are, and the sticks change on the whim of a judge or the price of a lawyer and the carrots might come but may not come and they change in size depending on the mood of a mob that society will not be very efficient or effective.

Chapter 23
Group Behavior is Sum of Individual Behavior

Insanity in individuals is rare but in groups nations and committees is the norm rather than the exception. Almost all large group behavior seems very illogical. People don't seem to be able to understand why groups behave the way they do, why groups do things to hurt the group. Why governments do what they do? Why governments do things that harm their people. It seems so complex but really it is incredibly simple to predict what any group or organization, committee or government will do.

You can tell exactly what any group will do by simply assuming every single individual in that organization will do exactly what profits them as individuals the most. If you want to know exactly what a factory will do then look at
what action will benefit the individual factory worker, what individual action will benefit the line manager, what individual action will benefit the vice president what individual action will benefit the president.

Look at what individual action, will benefit each single individual the most, they will then do that. Simply add up all those easy to predict individual actions and you will know exactly what the group will do. Group behavior is not difficult to understand or predict. In the above case, you will see exactly what the factory will look like. The fact that companies make poor cars that wear out sooner than they should is very logical and very predictable. That union workers will work as slowly and sloppily as possible. That company presidents will make as much money as possible 100 times what a line worker makes. These are all incredibly logical and predictable they are not crazy or unpredictable. Every piece of society, every piece of every company, every piece of every school, every single individual of a university, every piece of every corporation, every piece of the military. Look at it as basic individuals doing what is best for them and what we see is perfectly predictable.

Should females be 50% of combat troops? well if you are a female congress person trying to get reelected the answer is yes. If you are a man who has been shot and your fellow combat soldier needs to pick you up and carry you a mile the answer is no. Answer for each and every individual as if they are an unemotional 100% gaming matrix player and you will predict reality pretty well. Realize everyone is only being selfish and that's all there is.

The fact that the University football coach makes 10 times as much as the University president is of course predictable. A football coach brings in 10x as much money and is vastly more important to the school's reputation than the College president who no one knows or cares about. The College president could die tomorrow be replaced and no one would see any difference in the school.

I am so often perplexed by people that hold their hands up in the air and say why do we have 3 generations of people on welfare. Stupid, if one generation has lived successfully and comfortably on welfare why would not the 2nd generation do the same? If the 2nd generation has been so successful that they reproduced, had kids and they have survived why would the 3rd generation not do it. The fact you had one generation did it predicts that you will have two and three and so on. The very fact that you can have generations of people living on government handouts and producing healthy children who in turn reproduce at high rates shows it's viable successful way to make a living.

College costs is another area that is completely logical and predictable of course colleges are outrageously expensive they have been subsidized by the government with student loans the idea that college costs would go down when the price of entry is guaranteed by tax dollars is beyond foolish. It shows a complete lack of understanding about basic cause and effect. Colleges are at the situation now were only about 10% of their students are in STEM fields which are of any use to society. The universities job is to make money and grow it is not to make society better and you grow by offering easy, soft knowledge majors that anyone can get a student loan and go to school a pulse and a checkbook is all that is needed to go to college no IQ required. The examples are endless. Lawyers are not in the business of helping people or making sure society is fair. Remember everyone and every act is selfish.

How would a society look if every person making laws acted in their own self-interest. The answer: Just like it does now. Of course, lawyers want to make laws so complicated you need lawyers to interpret those laws. Never ask a barber if you need a haircut and never ask a lawyer if you need a new law. Everyone is acting in their own self-interest either consciously or unconsciously and even if you have an aberrational individual who does not work in their own self-interest they will not survive long. I know three lawyers who are morally good individuals I made the unfortunate decision to hire one once because he was a good guy I could trust. He was not a very effective lawyer. I am not sure if he is still in the lawyer business and the other two I know are not. Just like a male lion who did not kill the previous male's cubs those short lived unselfish acts will be removed from the gene pool or the business world. Just like the hard-working taxpaying honest guy who sacrifices himself and his family to the interests of the state instead of his own personal interest he will be removed from the gene pool also. A welfare cheat or prisoner who reproduces 10 kids will become the standard and the welfare social worker who now has more need for her job will increase and of course the police who need to watch these people their jobs will increase. Every person will act to increase their fitness. It is not the fitness of society or the good of all it is the good of the individual that drives the society.

People don't see to get this fact that you can accurately predict the consequences of implementing anything new, any government program, company policy etc. by just asking yourself what each selfish individual will do. There was a situation at a school that had a no bullying policy. Any form of bullying was to be targeted and stamped out of existence. Children were to be educated and trained not to bully and such. Well it didn't take long before being a bully was unprofitable but being bullied was very profitable. There were even situations where unpopular students, smelly stinky, rude, ugly, social outcasts who no one liked or wanted to socialize with were producing accusations of being bullied on the flimsiest of interactions. This brought in the intervention teams and conferences and such were implemented so stop this bullying and the bully and bully had conflict resolution involving other members of the class and popular students. These social outcasts never had so much power, prestige and attention. But one problem no one foresaw was it quickly became the easiest course of action to avoid these unpopular kids like the plague. They went from having a 10% satisfactory social life to zero. Never talking to them was safer and less risky than being accused of being mean. Now the cool kids did zero interactions with the unpopular students ostracized them much more and stopped talking all together if they entered the room. They never spoke around them or let them know when any activity was planned. It had become safer, less risky, more profitable to give the lonely kids zero attention. The Social Justice Warriors just assumed they would force the bullies to do something unprofitable and unselfish. The SJW's also thought the outcasts would do unselfish acts. Of course, the SJW's never did a self-reflection to see if they were doing a selfish act.

I will say that again. It is the good of the individual that determines how the collective will behave. The shape of every society, every group is determined by how the rules of the game are set up. If the rules of the game are set up so that the benefit to the individual is in line with the benefit to the group then society will achieve its stated goals. But if the most profitable action for the individual is to sabotage the stated mission of the group than that group will sabotage it's stated mission. If a society is set up so that the individual selfish actions hurt the group don't allow the group to accomplish its mission. Then that is what will happen the group will be hurt it will be dysfunctional. I cannot explain this too much even though it is so very simple.

No group acts in any other way except by its individual members acting with total 100% extreme selfishness. The Christian church, the Muslim church each individual member of that religion is acting with extreme selfishness and as long as the church was set up so that each member did what was in his or her individual best interest they accomplish their goal. This is one reason the Abrahamic religions have been so successful. Every member of those religions did what was absolutely best for him or her. Trying to avoid everlasting torture in hell or getting to heaven is all there is, the carrot or the stick. Hell is the ultimate stick and heaven is the ultimate carrot. So, if 10 units of sacrifice on earth gets you 1,000,000 units of pleasure for eternity and avoids 1,000,000 units of pain in hell for eternity, act as selfish as possible.

It should be noted that as soon as it became possible to question the carrot and the stick in Christianity then Christianity began to fall apart. As soon as it was not in the selfish best interest of the individual then Christianity lost its power. Islam still has great power over its members the ultimate carrot is paradise your 72 virgins for a martyr's death. The ultimate stick is you get stoned to death if you don't comply and act in the best interest of religion the best interest is spreading that religion has been intertwined with the best interest of the individual. I would predict that Islam if it goes the direction of Christianity where most of its members are actually semi atheists who don't believe in hell. Then Islam will lose its power. I have had this argument with my leftist collectivist commie friends who say look at history Christianity killed so many in the past. To which I always answer yes if a Christian today believed that by torturing you for 2 days he could save you from everlasting torture the most logical and kindest thing he could do is torture and convert you. Especially if it helped him get into heaven also. But a vast majority of so called Christians today really don't believe the bible they are semi atheists really and many Muslims are not quite there yet. Public questioning and debate will still get you killed by that group.

So, this chapter is very simple if you want an organization to do something then make it beneficial for every individual who will only act in their own selfish interest to behave in such a way that the individual accomplishes the group's goals. There will never be a case when the individual harms him or herself to accomplish the group's goals unless they have bought into a promise of paradise, everlasting life etc. I will state this one more time the individual will never not act selfishly so if you want a group, an organization, a government, a corporation, a committee, a nonprofit entity to accomplish something you must make it so that each individual working in that organization doing the most individually selfish actions imaginable accomplishes that mission.

And by the same reasoning if an organization is pretending to accomplish something which is not in its own self-interest, it is lying. This is no different than an angler fish or snapping turtle pretending to offer a grub to a fish. Or a leopard pretending its spots are the shadows of leaves. Or that a still snake is really a tree branch. Nature is full of examples of deception, it is the predator's way to sneak up using stealth and attack the prey. Every animal blends into its surroundings to prey on every other animal.

All nonprofit organizations, all religions, all salesmen, all governments are selling something. It is positively criminal to teach your children that the government is there to help them, or that the insurance company is there to protect them, or that the bank is there to help them save money or that the electric company is there to make sure they have lights, or that the real estate company is there so they have a home. That is like teaching your kids that the University is there to make sure they get a good education. Or that your employer is there to treat you fairly. That the news is there to inform you. That the car salesman wants you to have nice safe care. That the government is there to help you. As soon as people realize how things work they can free themselves from delusions, hypocrisy and see the world clearly and embrace reality. And after this happens you can see that in most cases you can have many interactions which are mutually beneficial. Perhaps not completely one sided like buying a car for a dollar or your employer paying you 10x your market value. But you can see reality and the world more clearly. And some people find that comforting.

Chapter 24
Vigilante Justice Is Best

I hope it is apparent by now that all individuals and groups committees and branches of government only serve themselves and nothing else. Every intelligent person given enough time will observe this fact especially in government. The famous quote from J.R.R. Tolkien illustrates this point very well.

"The older I get the more my political opinions lean more and more to Anarchy. The most improper job of any man is bossing other men. Not one in a million is fit for it, and least of all those who seek the opportunity".

Which is another problem in big government those who climb to the positions of power are least quailed to wield it fairly.

All the police departments and the judicial systems and the lawyers and the judges and the jails and the courts and the politicians are only selling something. They are only there to benefit themselves. If two friends get in a fist fight in a bar and they shake hands and are done with the fight that is how it will be settled, if no government existed. However, in modern America in many cases charges will be filed and even if the bar owner doesn't want to file charges and neither man wants to file charges. There will still be arrests made. The law will say the state of Texas versus person A. And the state of Texas versus person B as if they have committed some crime against the entire state. Each of those men will have to pay probably $10,000 in court costs and lawyer fees. The police will get paid. the defending lawyers will get paid. The public defender and or the public prosecutor will get paid. The men might get assigned community service and the people that supervise that community service will get paid. Or the two men might get some probation where they have to pay some more fines or they might get some jail time in which will be more money paid to jails. Those jails may or may not be privately owned but it makes really little difference to the people sitting in the jails.

I have heard arguments by people that for-profit jails are horrible because they encourage judges to assigned people to jail they might not otherwise and I've even heard of the cases where judges have owned stock money in the for-profit jails. However, this sort of ignores the fact that the state paid for judge by being a state employee in fact does own stock in the state-owned jail. The government likes to earn money just as much as a private business likes to earn money. A person sitting in jail doesn't know if his jail is owned by a corporation or a government both are an organization designed to take money out of his pockets. Both are organizations, designed to benefit themselves at the cost of another organization or organism. Both obey the laws of nature and grow at the expense of other things consuming resources it takes from others and growing.

Any time the government gets involved in disputes and becomes the 3rd 4th or 5th party in an incident which is so far removed from the actual grievance as to have no skin in the game, no care for the person being harmed. Their ox did not get gored and they are only there because of their paycheck and their pension and their medical plan which is not affected by a bad or unfair decision on their part. (so, they will just make the most self-serving action on their part.) A person dealing with this type of situation is very unlikely to receive any kind of justice.

At times, it is even possible that no grievance was committed. One person can claim a crime was committed against them, when no crime was committed and have the full weight of the government to attack the other person for them. Many experienced police will tell you that many of their calls, runs and resources are spent on annoying people calling for trivial reasons. Many weak, pathetic, people will call the cops for nothing the least imaginary infraction. This can go the other direction also. A person really harmed by another legally not allowed to take his own revenge is really left up to the whim of the government if they get justice or not. Just like harming person is up to the whim and luck of the government if they get punishment or not.

This is why I believe vigilante justice is the best justice. Actual vigilante justice, frontier justice, street justice which gets such a bad rap is the best type of justice. Of course, vigilante justice is not 100% fair but neither is our present system. If someone tries to rob someone and they get shot during the robbery that is wonderful according to some people. Other people think no individual has a right to protect their property and take someone's life unless they have a badge and government approval to take someone else's life. I don't really follow the logic that seems to be a common belief. I read a statistic that 80% of rapes the victim knows the perpetrator, I bet if the laws were changed so that a woman who got raped had every legal right to shoot the man the next day the number of rapes and go down. And I think there would be very few women indiscriminately killing men they disliked for whatever reason who did not actually rape them. If we had such a society and I heard in the news 300 miles from my house that some woman shot a man because he raped her on a date the previous night, I would figure it's none of my business probably he did and he deserved to be shot. Maybe he didn't and he was a victim but I would take those odds over our current legal system. I would be willing to bet that system would cause more rapists to be killed, less rapes to happen and more women satisfied with the justice system than what currently happens in our American justice system. Maybe men would be more careful dating Psycho bitches. Maybe Darwinism would take effect and clean up the gene pool.

The same can be said for spousal abuse. If a woman in some town in Kansas shot her husband of 10 years and said he beat me and I shot him. It's really not my business, maybe she's a murderer and did it for no good reason. Maybe he was a prick and deserved it. I will never know but the police will never know either, and that is the point. The only 2 people who know are the woman and her husband and one of them took care of it. And I don't even care if the husband was innocent and he was just stupid enough to pick a bad wife and stay with her for 10 years. People need to assume some responsibility and consequences for their bad choices. Again, if that system is in place I bet it would be fairer than we have now. We would have less domestic violence and it would certainly be less expensive. The actual number of spousal abuse would go down if someone realized if they beat their spouse and abused their spouse that their spouse had every right to shoot them. It would be actual justice. The percentage of bullies would go down.

The examples of this are many. We have protesters on the roads kicking cars and smashing windshields and the only reason they are not run over is because the people driving the cars are afraid of being arrested by the police. I have found it amazingly ironic that black lives matter protesters who block freeways and stop people freely moving on the road protesting against the police are only able to block freeways and protest because the police stop people from running them over. They are being protected and allowed to do this by the very police they are protesting against. The only reason they are safe to block the streets and threaten people is because the police allow them to block the streets and threaten people. We have law followers afraid of breaking the law and lawbreakers not afraid to break the law. The ones who don't care about breaking the law are rewarded and this is another example in the game of life, in the game of modern American politics. The cheaters are set up to win and the ones who follow the rules are set up to be punished they lose the game.

Now this of course is always argued well you can't have vigilante justice some people would be abused by the stronger or there would be a case of someone who broke into a house and just stole things and shot the people who live there. As if this doesn't happen all the time today with the police system set in place. If people breaking into houses had a 20% chance of being killed by the homeowner the odds of them doing it five times would be low. Almost everyone in jail for robbery will tell you that they have committed 20 robberies for every one that they got caught for. And just to make matters worse in our current justice system. For everyone that is in jail for burglary they have a list of about 20 burglaries on their record. That means they have committed 400 burglaries 20×20 before they ever really got put in jail. Any dog monkey or person can see that this is simply training people to steal if you let a dog crap on your floor 400 times and then hit them with a stick the 401 time you have not trained them to not shit on the floor. You have trained them to shit on the floor. In modern American society, we train people that it's

184

okay to rob. After they have served some time in jail networking with other criminals and learned new skills they will be released and probably start again. Prison is like a professional development workshop for law breakers. Get a thousand golfers to hang out and live together and not expect them to improve their golf game. Get a thousand lawyers to live together for a year and not expect them to make new contacts and network and improve in their business.

As can be seen with simple math vigilante justice is much fairer than our current system. Not only would it allow people to defend themselves. It would also encourage neighborhoods and families and communities and good people to work together to stand up against the thieves and criminals. Which is something the government absolutely does not want to happen. In the Trayvon Martin, George Zimmerman case. A Hispanic man who was a neighborhood watch captain who called 911 asking for assistance from the police. Was demonized by the entire nations politically correct narrative driven media politicians and even our President. Trayvon Martin who by all forensic evidence initiated the attack, the only bruise on his body was on his knuckles, Trayvon bashed George Zimmerman's head into the concrete and broke his nose and waited 3 minutes to circle back and attacking George from behind even though the house he was walking to his only 20 seconds away. It never occurred to the several people who said on national media several times that if George hunted down and shot this poor boy like an animal, George would be unmarked and not have called 911 in the first place. Trayvon never called 911 he called his girlfriend and said a creepy ass cracker was following him sounding annoyed. Trayvon's family was given millions of dollars by the neighborhood Association.

The way the bullet entered Trayvon's chest shows that his shirt was bloused downward and not against his chest proving he was sitting on George Zimmerman chest punching him when the gun went off. He could not have been laying on the ground underneath George when the gun went off because the shirt was not against his chest when the bullet entered his chest. The gun powder burns prove this. But none of this mattered because as if a giant conspiracy, a secret meeting, where everyone read the memo and agreed what the story would be happened. Every news outlet, every media anchor, every spokesman for every institution, condemned this evil white man for killed an innocent 12-year-old boy. It did not matter that none of this was true it was played on the TV all day and all night. The news networks edited the tapes taking Georges words out of order and context and even removing words between his sentences to misrepresent what he said. How could this happen? It was so fast, so well organized, so coordinated, everyone seemed to be on the same page of the play book. Even the president and justice department and full weight of billions of dollars of power pushed this narrative. The fact that Trayvon had a burglary tool in his school locker with 13 women's rings was of course kept out of the media. It didn't fit the big government narrative.

Now imagine a different America, one in which the government was tiny and people in neighborhoods were encouraged to form watch groups and see who was coming in their neighborhoods. Careful of people unknown and who didn't belong there. If every person owned their home and didn't have to pay any property taxes on it and was going to stay in their neighborhood for a long time they would have a huge interest in protecting their neighborhood they would be on the lookout for people trying to rob their neighborhoods this might really make it unprofitable to be a robber. Neighborhoods might be so safe and secure the children can walk down the streets with little worry. Little old ladies could carry their purses dangling from their shoulders. But as it now stands people get many chances to rob, second chances, third chances, fourth chances even after their only caught which only happens about one out of every 20 times. Making it much more profitable, much safer, much lower risk to rob houses that it is to start your own business and risk going bankrupt legally. If you are a burglar and case a neighborhood walking around in the rain looking into people's houses for a possible business opportunity and a neighborhood watch caption sees you and calls 911 and does what the police say. (see something say something) and you wait, walk around the neighborhood wait, stalking that guy for 4 minutes jump him from behind smash his head in the ground and get shot trying to kill him. You get made a hero and your family gets millions of dollars that is a pretty good indication of who the government is trying to help.

People always use terrible illogical examples of why frontier justice, or vigilante justice will not work. They always pick examples of a country that had a strong oppressive government, that oppressed its people and finally collapsed and has 4 or 5 different government factions fighting for control as an example of anarchy. They say see this is what you get without government. Well that is what you get with failed government and with governments fighting over control but it isn't an example of a stable society with very little, government control. Many societies in the past has a very hands off, live and let live, let the local street justice run things and we will not spend all the resources to get in everyone's business which ran comparatively well. The comparisons are difficult to make because as a society gets richer it tends to grow the government which then correlates a big government with a rich prosperous society which is a correlation but not a causation.

One final example I will use is a more personal one. When I talk to older people I am surprised at the number or percent who have a story similar to this. My great grandmother was an orphan she was not wanted at birth or her mother or father were ne'er-do-wells and she was raised by an uncle or aunt or some other member the family. Before the days of birth control and child protection services, and welfare, and state assistance, and children being given to the state, children taken in as wards of the state, or children taken into foster care and given to complete strangers. In the old days, most children would die if some member of their extended family didn't care for them. This is sort of like vigilante justice because even though I'm sure the situation was far from ideal in the past and there was most probably abuse. I would bet that it was still better than what we have today. The statistics on children put in foster care is something like 20 times more likely to be abused then with their biological families. The lure of government money to foster care families has made it profitable for predatory people to start a business taking in children who are wards of the state. And what kind of good family person wants to bring in other children to their own children who have all kinds of problems. Imagine you have 2 or 3 beautiful healthy children of your own. Do you would you want to bring in another who may sexually abuse them, who may have developed predatory habits and introduce this into your happy harmonious home? What kind of person does that?

Only a person with a hidden agenda finds this situation attractive and most often just like in modern politics where the people most unfit to lead want to lead. We have a situation with the people most unfit to parent the states children wanting to parent.

Chapter 25
No Society is Best for Everyone

There seems to be in modern political discussions an idea that is returned to repeatedly. I hear this from leftist frequently. Which basically says: If we could only have more socialism, more communism, more cooperation then we would have a much better society. Basically, the concept is, if everyone would just act unselfish, if everyone would only do what's best for the group, then everything would be better for the group. And the best way to do that is to make the government so big and so powerful that it makes forces everyone to cooperate. If we could just force or train or brainwash or make everyone unselfish then we would have a better society.

This seems to actually be the only argument the left has. And it is based on the impossible.

It ignores that deciding who will rule over people with such force only gives more power to those who want to rule over people the most who are the ones who should least have that power. The people who get the power are precisely the people least likely to rule kindly and gently.

It ignores that the people who want to rule over others are doing it only for selfish reasons and while everyone is selfish some are greedier than others and more cruel.

It also has the problem of assuming and this is the point of this chapter, that there is one way to rule that helps everyone the most. It assumes that there is one set of instructions, one way to create society that helps everybody. That there is one common good. Anyone with a brain can see that if you change the game you reward certain strategies and punish others. This just like that there is no such thing as the perfect society for everyone. There is no such thing as the best society for everyone. This is obvious if someone is a mentally challenged 60 IQ person living in free society that requires every person to take care of themselves that person would not be well off. They would be better off in a society that required everyone to pool their money together and take care of them. A high IQ healthy person would be better off in a more Darwinian society that did not take his money to care for less fit others.

The question is not what society is best, For Everyone. That is a limited question it's a question of who in society will be helped and who in society will be hurt. Because it's impossible to help everyone. No rule changes helps everyone, no law helps everyone, no new tax helps everyone. The real question is, what kind of society do you want to have. What kind of behavior do you want to encourage. Who do we want to benefit and who do we want to disadvantage. There is no other way to address this topic. The smokescreen of we want to help everyone, and have no one disadvantaged is such a lie. The question of how will society be structured and who are the targets that society wants to benefit is what must be brutally asked.

I have a liberal hippie socialist brainwashed globalist friend who was trying to explain to me the concept of a "common good". This is an idea that there is one course of action "good for everyone" or "good for all". That there is one game with its set of rules that benefits everyone. I tried to explain that this was simply untrue. That nothing benefits everyone. He used the example that public education as good because it helped everyone. I shot that idea down so even he could see that didn't help everyone. He then said a minimum wage was for the common good for which I gave several counter examples. Finally, in exasperation he said fine I will give you an example even you can't argue with. Everyone should have good eyesight and that it was in everyone's best interest to have good eyesight. And that if anyone was blind it was harmful to the overall good of that society. I explained to him that even this was not true. If all the child molesters and baby rapists in that society were blind it would be very good for babies and children. He was stunned. I said No if all human predators were blind it would be good for society. If all muggers and burglars were blind it would help homeowners and walkers. That was difficult for him to acknowledge. He kept going back to his Communist Party line that there was such a thing as the common good for everyone. That if everyone ate breakfast that was good, that if everyone had healthcare that was good. That all children being taking care was good and that was good for everyone. I explained to him that this was not true because my wife and I only had two children because we were responsible and that's how many children we could care for ourselves but his government stole money from my wife and I and gave it to women who squirted out 10 kids and could not take care of any of them. So, in his mind those 10 kids being taking care of because they outnumbered my two kids is an example of the common good. I explained to him that no, it was not good. His dream society has murdered any of my potential children that I did not have because I chose not to have them because I could not afford to have them. If the government did not take so much money from me in the form of taxes. My wife and I could afford to have one or two more children so we might have three or four children instead of two but this was taken from us so the government basically killed two of my kids. He laughed and said this of course was not true because you can't kill somebody who never lived. I said you're right, my potential children never even got a chance to live under your system of the common good for everybody. My wife and my two children or four would be better off in a society that let those other ten kids die. So, no your example is bad for my family.

He then went on and said well there is the argument of balance of pain in society, for example if a million-people had a migraine head ache or one person was killed what would be better? He seemed to think that a million-people suffering a head ache was better for the common good than one person dying. And I said no. There is no common good. If you are one of the million with a bad migraine headache it would be better to kill the stranger and not suffer headaches but if you were the one being killed it would be better to let a million have head aches and you live. There is no common good. Its only what's best for the individual not the whole. And he said no it would be better for everyone to have a headache than to have one person killed? It seems that these collectivists indoctrinated people never tire watching other people sacrifice for the good of everyone else. I asked him if he had cancer cells in his body if he would cut them out or would he want the common good of all the cells. His cancer cells and body cells are all cells of his body doesn't he want them all to survive. Or was he going to pick and choose which of his cells to help and which of his cells to harm.

You see every decision is selfish and there is no common good for everyone. There is only the good for who you want to benefit and harm for who you want to hurt. For some reason, many people want to benefit certain groups and cut out others. Just like they would like to benefit their own cells and cut out the cancer.

Why don't most Leftists consider their own cancer cells which are their own cells deserving of life and work for their benefit? They are after all cells from their bodies and just as entitled to the benefits of their body as the rest of their selves. They pick and choose what the common good is for their body and it usually does not include the cancer cells. Now the argument might be because the cancer cells are consuming more than their fair share of resources and out breeding the other cells and are creating an unsustainable situation which is unstable and cannot last. Well I would say the welfare state government handouts are very similar. But since the pain is slow and only future generations will suffer the most self-interested most selfish course of action is to simply vote for more handouts and keep the politically correct party line going, and let future generations of the children pay for it.

Chapter 26
Beta Males, Feminists and Protected Ones

As can be seen from the previous chapter when their life is on the line people will choose to cut out the cancer cells and really don't believe in the common good at all. But at other times they want to give a special designation to different cells and provide extra resources for them. Why are some groups favored over others? Why do certain groups get preferential treatment over others? Why does an Asian have to score 400 points higher on their SAT to get into the same college as an African? Why is it all right to discriminate against some members of the society but not others? Isn't the aim of the government to make everything fair and equal? Why can a baker who refuses to bake a wedding cake for a gay marriage have his business destroyed by the government but a baker who refuses to bake a wedding cake for a Nazi marriage allowed to? Obviously, the government is not trying to make anything fair or equal. That very question shows a lack of logic.

If everyone were treated equally, the situation would be unfair. Imagine if we did affirmative action in all areas. Imagine if in the NBA or the NFL we said; no matter what the stopwatch said in the 40-yard dash time we were going to impose racial quotas on the outcomes making them equal. That would be unfair. You can have fair and unequal or you can have equal and unfair. But you cannot have both.

Remember everyone is just seeking to maximize their own profit and everyone's actions are 100% selfish. So, when a male claims to be a feminist he is not being a self-sacrificing, altruistic male he is maximizing his own self-interest. I have scanned through pictures of feminist rallies and seen male participants. In 99% of those cases those weak, sissy, Beta males would never be able to compete with other males. The only niche they have that they can successfully exploit is with the females. But not with traditional females who are seeking an alpha male but only beta females who could never actually attract an alpha male. These women pretend men get paid more for the exact same job and demand equal pay? Even though that has been a law since 1963 and they can produce no actual case where it is happening.

Today the universities are sanctuaries for the incompetent and dysfunctional. How many college professors could score high in mathematics, physics, chemistry, geology, biology or any of the hard sciences? Our colleges are full of PhD professors in soft knowledge areas with very ordinary IQs. Many of them simply came from a privileged background that allowed them to stay in school and never actually get a job to support themselves. It is interesting to note that it is in this environment that the social justice warrior has risen to such prominence. Many of the socialist, left leading college professors are the exact thing they rage against. Perhaps it is some kind or guilt for their privilege and they think all people had this growing up like they did.

Men who could not fix a car, roof the house or wire lamp now are considered experts of fields of knowledge and held in the highest regard. It is in the basic self-interest of these people to promote their collectivist agenda and that is why they do it.

Remember everyone is simply seeking to maximize their own profit and it is in the best interest of the weak male, who is after all a beta male, to promote an environment that values Beta males. It is in the best interest of an unattractive or even repulsive female to blame all her problems on the patriarchy and seek extra advantages and special treatment for her group. I have seen studies which showed the physical appearance dichotomy between female Hillary Clinton voters and female Donald Trump voters in 2016.

It is also interesting to note that anyone who is rich and powerful and already made it is in their best interest to destroy all competition and make sure the talented do not rise to compete with them. It is in their best interest to promote the less talented members of society. Imagine you are rich and established in a business. Wouldn't you like a very closed, non-free market government restricting environment to stop any young talented brilliant young entrepreneurs from springing up to compete with you. Therefore, established businesses love anti-business governments

One game that mother nature plays is called Lekking. This is when multiple males compete for females in open display and combat. This is a rather straightforward game and simple in its outcome. The biggest, strongest, fastest, most coordinated males put their skills on display and when breeding rights to the most females. Theoretically these bigger, stronger faster, superior males will pass these traits onto the offspring and the female by combining her genes with these alpha males has made the most profitable decision for herself. However just like in human governments cheating can occur. Nature provides several examples of sneaky Beta males avoiding head-to-head competition with alpha males just like we see in American Government. One of the most famous examples is the cuttlefish. The strongest male cuttlefish flash bright colors and display their power and might offering to fight with other males in open combat while the females go to the seafloor waiting to mate with the winner. But over time this system has been defeated, small weak Beta males have learned to tuck in their tentacles and not show bright colors and then swim past the males pretending to be females. They then join the females waiting to see who the winning male might be and mate with them. These sneaky, deceptive, beta males are now more successful than the alpha males in spreading their genes. I don't know what the long-term effects of this will be. It is likely that the strongest best fighting male cuttlefish will also produce the strongest fastest swimming cuttlefish who can capture the most prey. It would probably be in the best interest of the female to select a stronger healthier male than the weaker deceptive male but maybe there just hasn't been time for the females to have developed any counter to this yet. It may be over time as the females who are bred by the weaker slower males produce weaker slower offspring who are not able to capture as much prey and so produce fewer offspring and over millions of years this may lead to a situation where females who are choosy and reject the beta males are more successful and outcompete the other females thus removing deceptive male's genes from the population. But this would require a great deal more study it would be interesting to make a computer model and play out simulations and guess how long it would take the gene to be removed from the population or to even use such a computer simulation to guess how long this cheating behavior has existed in the population that is the difference study and a topic for another more specialized book. The cuttlefish example is well known because cuttlefish are so flamboyant and so colorful and so easily noticed but cheating occurs any time it is profitable.

Male antelope who have a female antelope in their territory will actually bark fake warning calls pretending a leopard or lion is nearby scaring the female to stay with him longer so he can mate with her more and monopolize her from other competing males. Hippies who think mother nature is in any way more noble in human beings can see that this behavior is no different than a man pretending he has a better job than he does to gain access to a female. Or a human female putting on makeup and a push-up bra to pretend she is more attractive than she really is to get favor from a human male. Each is doing what profits them the most, being 100% selfish and dishonest as they can possibly, get away with. I had a former student who came back as an adult and talk to me and explained how he infiltrated politically leftist groups in college to gain access to the females. He was very right winged politically but said to me with a smile a man has to do what a man has to do to get laid.

I would clump these feminists, beta males, and social justice warrior's, in fact anyone who fights for special privileges for one group over another is simply an example of this cheating behavior which is simply a selfish act of maximize profit for that individual's group. Take special note, it is often in a person's best interest to work for the special privileges of another group. For example, a white professor who has tenure is benefitted by any affirmative action which blocks other whites from becoming a professor. A white student already enrolled in a college would be very selfishly benefitted by admissions that blocked other whites from getting into university. A rich person who had an established business and mansion and body guards for his kids is benefitted by gun laws that stop the average person from owning a gun to protect his home.

Another interesting example of how complex the beta behavior can become was a study I read long ago of tree frogs. Apparently, in this species of frog males set up territories and defended them against other males. The bigger and stronger the male the bigger and better territory he could occupy and the more females he would have in his territory to mate with. But much like the cuttlefish beta males would try to sneak in and pretend to be females however the alpha males would recognize them and kicked them out and so the beta males had no breeding success. However, scientists noticed that one group of this frog developed a super male who was bigger and stronger than the alpha male and could beat them up and push them out of their territory. This aberrational super male could monopolize all the breeding rights to females and would drive the alpha males to extinction. But this did not happen it seems these super males could be tricked by the beta males into treating them like females. This was like what happened to the cuttlefish. The researchers reported that it was like a game of rock, paper, scissors. The alpha males would dominate smashing out the smaller weaker males. But once a super male appeared he would beat up and drive out the alpha males and gain control of the breeding grounds. Until the sneaky beta males would infiltrate his territory and breed all the females driving his kind to extinction. After time, the beta males would be infiltrated by alpha males who would drive them to extinction. who would then in turn be driven out by the super males and so on and so forth. The examples of creative ways to cheat the game are nearly endless and is again one reason why no government with its slow legislation drafting of bills to be voted on to become laws will never keep up with individuals quickly adapting their behavior to cheat the system. No group given special protection, or special privilege, or favored status can ever help themselves but exploit it and take advantage of it.

Groups given special privileges and protections always lead to tyranny.

Chapter 27
Jealously, Envy and Class Division

Jealousy is a such a strong driving force of humanity that it is even mentioned in the Bible. "You shall not covet your neighbor's house. You shall not covet your neighbor's wife, or his male or female servant, his ox or donkey, or anything that belongs to your neighbor." This is very good advice. Even the great Nietzsche talks about envy although he has a different almost opposite take on it. Suggesting that you should embrace your envy own up to it for it is a sign you should do better and be more. Either way or both ways envy is a driving force of human behavior.

Envy is the driving force behind communism, socialism and is a major tool used by the big government collectivists. The jealous and envy of people is a driving force wanting to tax the rich. Even the word progressive tax means attacking and punishing some people more than others. Why isn't that called regressive. A flat income tax would be fair. Everyone pay 10% of their income. But this cannot pass because everyone wants to punish those who make more than them. Laws and government are not fair because one of the largest driving forces behind all human motivation is not fairness but jealousy. If people think a law puts someone else at a disadvantage they will accept it. As long as a government program penalizes someone "else" people will accept it. The world shudders at this human motivation it is the root cause, motivating force behind so much crime.

In Russia, early 1900s the most successful farmers who rose to middle class were torn to shreds murdered, and destroyed by those who had less. In china, the same thing happened. In Cambodia, the same thing. In the United states in the early 2000s we have the same thing certain groups are considered evil just by belong to that group. I have heard Academic tax supported people saying, all men are misogynist and all white people are racist. I have heard tax supported government sanctioned speakers saying only white people can be racist and we must fight racism. Which translates to we must fight white people. We must end racism, only whites can be racist means we must end white people.

Jealousy is one of the most efficient, powerful and primal ways that the government deceives and manipulates people. I watched an experiment were a monkey did a behavior and was given a slice of cucumber. The monkey did the behavior again was given the slice of cucumber. Then the monkey did it again and they got another slice of cucumber. The monkey was very happy to receive this reward every single time and then the experimenter had a 2nd monkey in the cage next to the first monkey and when that 2nd monkey did the behavior that monkey was given a grape. And when the researcher had the first monkey do behavior again and handed it a cucumber slice the monkey flew into a rage and threw it against the wall. The cucumber slice was no longer a reward it hated the cucumber it wanted the grape as a reward just like the monkey beside it got. It was quite startling to see the violence of the first monkey who had been so clearly and perfectly satisfied with slices of cucumber before.

Jealousy and class envy shown by this monkey in this experiment was quite dramatic and I don't think people have evolved past this one little bit. The government can use this class warfare deception on its citizens to an amazing degree to control their behaviors. Again, this is not because of some central committee newsletter was read or agreed to by a conspiracy group. It is simply part of the politically correct narrative that anyone must follow and accept if they are going to rise into a position of power and influence, and no one rises to those positions without towing the politically correct party line.

This is one reason the government must use identify politics to keep everyone at each other's throat and busy fighting each other and constantly jealous of each other. America used to be called a great melting pot. This meant that every culture came together and melted i.e. was gone and melted into and became something new American. This idea is now discouraged Government schools now teach that idea is wrong. Imagine a homogenous American culture of people united in questioning their government. However, a population that is 5% Christian and 5% Muslim and 5% Gay and 5% liberal and 5% conservative and 5% Jew and 5% atheist and 5% etc. all fighting with each other each so jealous of each other will never get together and cooperate long enough to look behind the curtain.

The class warfare is amazingly effective at keeping a government in power. There are even groups wanting reparations paid for a whole group of people punishing people who did no crime. Never in any type of law has it been suggested that an innocent group has committed no crime be punished. Imagine if all the Americans of Italian ancestry were charged with a slavery tax by Americans of English ancestry for crimes committed by the Roman empire. It is so preposterous that one wonders how the idea has gotten as far as it has. Well one reason for this is class envy and jealousy. Humans love to take from anyone who seems to have an advantage

No one roots for Goliath. This is an old saying and like most stereotypes and clichés often true. Many people secretly hope the champion will fall. Many people love to see the dominate team lose. Let a person win the lottery and tax him to death so he can't get too far ahead. Let someone get a nice house tax him severely even if it hurts you to pay taxes on your house. This is why politicians who are all millionaires must hide their wealth. Movie stars must hide the fact that they are not common people. The mob does not like anyone who gets ahead of them.

Identify politics, class warfare, is too powerful of a human motivation to ignore. This is one reason the idea of white privilege is sold to America to cause the most powerful of emotions jealousy, envy, resentment. The Government must have a victim and an oppressor to pit against each other. This game is very simple. Always cast the most numerous, dominate powerful group as the oppressor. This way it is always under attack and energy is spent fighting it. In the United States, today. Christians are the dominate religion so they are the oppressor and must be attacked. Whites are the strongest race so they must be attacked. Heterosexual people are the most common so they must be attacked. This method insures no group will become a monopoly. If the day comes when Muslims are the dominate religion then they might be attacked to weaken them. Or if Jews became the dominate religion than they might be attacked. The best strategy is to have no cohesive group. If America has a whole bunch of fragmented groups jealous, envious, distrusting, fighting, working against each other this ensures the Government will stay large and in charge. We need the big government to protect us from those other groups and keep them in line.

Chapter 28
Your Brother's Keeper

This whole Idea which so permeates our thinking that it is even a famous bible verse. Think of the destruction this meme has caused. Drug laws, every person in jail for marijuana possession being raped and tortured but it was only done for their own good. Think of every child truant from school captured by the truant officer and put in a boy's home to be abused but it's only done for their own good. The examples of people making draconian laws or actions because they assume they should be there Brother's keeper is colossal.

I ran for state representative once and freely tried to debate everyone who would debate with me. I developed a standard answer when debating Christians who wanted to make abortion illegal because they the mother didn't know how to make the right decision. Or gambling illegal because they wanted to protect the gambler from himself. Or wanted the county to be dry so no one could buy alcohol because they would protect the alcoholic from himself. To these people and all their arguments, I would say one tenet of Christianity is God gives human beings free will. That is the explanation for God allowing all the horrible things humans do to be done. Murders, rape, robberies, violations, etc. and I would always say to these people. "If God allows people to have free will why do you assume you know more than God" "Why should you want to exercise more power in people's lives and more influence in people's lives than God Almighty."

Now I know this argument should only work on Christians, and many of the leftists, socialist, big government types are atheists. But they are really not atheists they are State theists they have simply substituted the state for their God. They are just as religious, just as zealous, its simply they now worship the State.

So that every human behavior the fundamentalist Christians wants to entrust in the name of God to curb and control is exactly the same behavior the Stateatheists want to entrust in the state to curb and control. The two are not opposites. They are really, almost identical they just bow down to different gods. The idea or concept that you know better how another person should act and behave for themselves than they know how to act or behave for themselves is arrogant beyond belief. It is and arrogant intrusive and overreaching god or an arrogant intrusive and overreaching state, same thing. The amount of abuse dealt out to individuals by others in the guise of helping them assuming the cloak of deception that they are there Brother's keeper and they are only doing it for another's own good justifies everything up to murder and even genocide. There is maybe no more effective camouflage for a predator to use in modern government than I am doing this to help that group. This is the same throughout history. The Spanish Inquisition was a group trying to save the heathen from himself. The Communists in China in the 1950s were going to save the people from themselves. Stalin in the 1920s was doing this for the good of the workers saving them. When religion gets big enough, when a corporation gets big enough it becomes government. Google is heading in that direction now.

Why does every person you ask no matter their political identity laugh when you say the quote "I'm from the government and I'm here to help you"

Chapter 29
Society can be Planned,
Just how Close to Utopia can we get?

This is where the rubber meets the road.
This is the meaning of the phrase the devil is in the details.
I hope I have convinced the reader that no real society populated by individuals who only and always seek maximum profit for themselves can match the theoretical dream of everyone sacrificing and trying to spread their money and their profit around to everyone else. This is just reality.

In the previous chapter I stated a theoretical game saying if everyone cooperated every turn of the cards, everyone would come away with 7 points. The theoretical optimum strategy, the one of most good for the most. However, this is not the actual sustainable strategy this is pretending you have transparent cards and can see the future as if which card they are holding and which card they will play. This is the imaginary society we could have if everyone would just work hard and share and read each other's mind. (which the government I'm sure is working on) It is as "imaginary" as a perfect engine with no waste heat or the perfect black box model in physics. 7 was the maximum profit that the sum of everyone in the game could get if everyone always cooperated. That is unachievable in real life. And the more we try to force it up to 7 by rules, regulations, watchers, guards, added taxes and layers of Bureaucracy the farther it drops from 7.

The game I described in the beginning was arbitrary I assigned each player 7 points if they both play cooperate and 10 points to the winner if he played betray and the other played cooperate which really doesn't make cheating that profitable. If you want to make cheating occur more frequently simply assign 5 points for both cooperate and 10 points for betrayal. Any society or any system that is designed in which cheating or taking advantage would be a benefit is unstable. Because you are rewarding cheating, and cheating will occur whenever it is profitable to do so. You cannot make a system that rewards cheating and not have cheating occur. Which our current government does. Remember from a previous chapter you cannot offer a resource and expect that resource to not be exploited. So how close can we get to the theoretical maximum? My conclusion is that if we set up a system that rewards cooperation, discourages cheating, and maximizes the individuals reward for his effort, we will get the most profitable system for the most. It is interesting again to see a system that was very much like this in the past. Compare the articles of piracy to a modern business. Any logical person looking at a gaming matrix that had as its values the boss makes 1000 times what the employee does, if the boss makes a bad decision and destroys the company, he suffers zero consequences, employees have absolutely no recourse to punish a bad boss. A logical person would predict that such a game would produce exactly what we have in modern America.

This is where it gets interesting society can be planned, customized like a fine tailored suit we just must decide what we want. What do we want life to mean? If we want life to mean live with honor, tell the truth, be loyal, be true, faith, love etc. then we must make a society where those things are profitable and not doing those things is unprofitable. It cannot happen otherwise. There is no other way to achieve the outcomes.

Another point is if we want the system to survive it must be stable. Many societies in the world today held up as examples of success are going extinct, they will not last. They are like the big strong athlete who smokes and does cocaine he can do that for a little while and still dominate but it is not sustainable. A stable society is not a theoretical utopia which rewards cheating but a society set up that does not reward cheating. Breaking the agreed upon rules cannot be rewarded i.e. cheating is unprofitable. This will be the highest value payout that can be achieved in the real world which has individuals with free will.

I would guess that although a theoretical 7 would be impossible I bet we could get to about a 6.5 average payout, which is about maximum for humans and higher than any country especially communist, socialist countries have ever achieved. Ant and termite society have a higher payout but have done away with free will. Which many social justice warriors, collectivists, Communists, Socialists, state atheists see as a goal for human beings. If google could only track every human, monitor their writings and opinions, read their diaries, look at their families and know their most personal thoughts feelings and beliefs. It is interesting that I believe some fully brainwashed religious societies based on the reward of heaven and the abject terror of hell could come close to the insect world's payout. This might be one reason why extreme religious adherence societies have spread so fast and outcompeted and dominated less religious societies. Maybe the modern Statetheist is headed in that direction.

Humans can have almost any type of society they want. They can create almost any society except a utopian communistic, socialist one that rewards the very traits which hamper society. This is because the very rules put in place to increase profit, decrease that profit. The very rules put in place to decrease pain and suffering, increased pain and suffering. My suggestion is that the most productive, creative, safest, fairest, wealthiest, society would be one that maximizes freedom and in no way rewards undesirable behavior or traits such as stupidity, laziness, irresponsibility, victim hood, poor parenting, not caring for your children, lying, cheating, dishonor bullying etc. Now which traits does modern American government subsidize?

In the best society those harmful traits would be punished quickly and efficiently and the beneficial traits rewarded. The best, most cost-effective way to do that is not to assign government punishment squads and pay them to monitor people. It would be to do it like has always been done in the past and let nature take its course and allow Darwinism to take effect. The most efficient, effective behaviors would give the highest profit for each individual improving and rewarding him.

We must also allow local justice. If a woman is beaten by her husband for nothing and she shoots him that is not anyone else's business. I would be willing to sign a marriage contract with my wife that said if she shoots me I don't want anyone to prosecutor if you don't love and trust someone that much don't marry them. And if you do make a poor judgment and get killed by your spouse I am willing to chalk that up to you did improper selection of a mate and deserved what you got. But I certainly don't want my tax dollars, my profit, my children's piano lessons, my family's resources going to pay to get vengeance for your stupidity. The same with a two business partners if one cheats the other and is killed for it that will eliminate cheating. The only way one business partner can cheat another safely is to do the cheating and then jump behind the protection of the law. On a personal note, I have seen several people have falling outs with her business partner and with 100% of these cases it was the sneaky lying cheating son of a bitch who use the law to fleece his partner and avoid any retaliation. In every case I witnessed the law allowed and helped and protected the cheater not the other way around.

I have also seen this happen in many divorce cases where the more evil, treacherous partner won in the courts. I have seen this in personal lawsuits where one person could not get their property from the other. Everyone seems to have a story like this of someone cheating them and they can't do anything about it, because of the law. And in each of these cases it does not seem to matter to the statetheists that this often happens because the intentions were good. People can always be abused and sacrificed to the state just like old Aztecs sacrificed to the sun god. Religious zealots always are happy to sacrifice other people to their gods. They will continue to pretend that if we could just do communism a little better it would reach the magical 7 points payout for everyone. Which is no different than people pretending the earth is 6,000 years old.

I do not understand people's ability to ignore reality and embrace a fantasy. These intellectuals in the universities that love socialism and would laugh at someone who thought the universe was 6,000 years old cannot seem to understand that what they theorize about it is just as unreal. Physicists and engineers don't seem to have the same problem they theorize about the ideal but know it is not applicable to the real world. A gas engine is far from its theoretical 100 percent efficiency, a real working engine will not even come close but it is a good model to make calculations from.

Chapter 30
Best Society Possible for who

Life really is what we make it, and society is what the government makes it. The only question is who do we make society for? We have already established that there is no such thing as a best society for everyone. And there is no universal good. There is no such thing as the best for everyone the question is who is society going to be good for and what type of person is society going to produce. If you have a society where a certain race gets extra points on their college entrance exam. Only certain sexual orientations get special protections under the law and special treatment. Then that society makes it profitable to be in those groups and disadvantageous to be in other groups.

As Voltaire said if you wish to see who rules over you simply ask who you cannot ridicule. Simply ask who you cannot criticize and then you know rules over you. The same could be said about society if you want to know who society is set up to benefit simply ask who you cannot criticize. Whatever that group is that you cannot criticize is the one society is set up to benefit, protect and promote. Likewise, the group that can be made fun of and ridiculed is the one it is not profitable to be. If we remove the idea of good and evil. And simply realize that everyone will act to maximize their profit. Everyone will seek the carrot and avoid the stick then we must ask what type of behavior gets the carrot and what type of behavior gets the stick.

If people want a society with honor, truth, loyalty, personal responsibility, where nice guys finishing first, help their neighbor, keep their word, don't steal, don't bully, are hardworking etc., then we must set up the game so that the desired behavior is profitable. A society must know the difference between protecting its weaker members and promoting its weaker members. A society must know the difference between taxing or slightly punishing its stronger more productive members and punishing them so much that they change their behavior to the more advantageous behavior. So, the question of what is the best society is incomplete. The real question is what is the best possible society for whom? If you want to make that society the best possible society for dumb people, lazy people or hard-working people or smart people or thieves or honest people or cheating people you must make the game, the society, the rewards, and punishments such that the people you want to promote are helped, are rewarded, are benefited, get the carrot and the people you want to not help, not promote, not encourage, get the stick, the punishment, the disadvantage.

I find it funny when people say we all have universal values and we all know what the best society should be. That is absolutely false we don't have universal values. Some people want horse thieves hung some people want a thief to have their hand cut off and never do it again some people want a thief to steal 10 times and still not get killed. Some people want the death penalty for robbery or murder some people don't want the death penalty ever. Some want Sharia law it would be the best for them. Some don't want Sharia law it would be the worst for them. Some want everyone to speak only English. Some want everyone to speak only Spanish. Some want everyone to speak Hawaiian. Some want everyone to speak Swahili. Some claim to want 2 languages a bilingual society. But this is a lie which two? Why not 3 or 4 or 6?

There is no one society that is the best for everyone. So, when societies are created and organizations are created people must decide how those organizations are going to be run. What the gaming matrix will be and what values are placed on what behaviors. They first must decide what they value. And they must make sure everyone is on the same page as to what their society is going to reward and promote and what it is going to punish and discourage. This is one problem with diverse conflicting cultures trying to form a single cohesive society. You can't have women with the right to vote and not with the right to vote. You can't give homosexuals more rights than heterosexuals and also throw them off buildings. There is no society that is the best society for everyone. There is only the best society for a certain type of person. And the culture is deciding what type of person what single direction is valued.

It gets even more confusing as sometimes people point to a dying society as a successful society but it just hasn't had enough time to die yet. A rich society that is rewarding all the things that will make it poor and punishing all the things that made it rich and doing all the things that will make it die. This society might still be a rich society for a while but it will not stay a rich society it is heading towards poverty and perhaps extinction. A society that is stable that can maintain itself must reward the things that will maintain itself and punish the things that will destroy it. It is really that simple. Today we see many societies rewarding things that will destroy it actually promoting the things that will destroy it and because it takes many years for a society to die people are touting that as a success as proof that destructive behavior isn't destructive. I know it's unbelievable and crazy. Except when you apply gaming theory and realize each selfish individual is acting only for themselves and this sum total of individual selfish behavior all added up is the groups behavior.

We have as many different ideas about what the best possible government is as we do different people. Some people think a government where everyone is taken care of no matter how lazy, how stupid or how evil, is the best form of government. Some people think government where the evil, stupid and lazy are removed so they cannot parasitize the smart, hard-working and generous is the best form of government. Some people think a government that governs the least governs the best. In this government which is close to natural selection or Darwinism there are few artificial interferences by the government. Some people think a government that interferes the most is best. Some people think the best government is the one that promotes their religion. Some people want their religion to be tax-exempt. Some people want public funds to teach their religion in schools. These public funds of course are taxes stolen so there really isn't such a thing as pubic funds. Some people think the best government would allow businesses to incorporate and have certain advantages over individuals for example a corporation cannot be sued or the Corporation get special rights or the Corporation doesn't have to follow the same laws as an individual. These people think business should be dominant to the individual. It is interesting that these people are almost the same as the communists and socialists who simply want that Corporation to be so large and powerful that we call it a Government.

The question what is the perfect government should really be rephrased what is the perfect government for YOU. or What is the perfect government for who? The answer always depends on what you want to promote and what you want to discourage. If you want a government that encourages laziness stupidity, irresponsibility, helplessness, victimhood, weakness, all you have to do is reward those behaviors. If you want a society that encourages hard work intelligence personal responsibility strength self-sufficiency all you have to do is reward those behaviors.

As a last note for a society or government to sustain itself and maintain itself it must be stable and many governments today many cultures today are dying and may be extinct in the next 100 years as they reward behaviors that lead to their own destruction. Because promoting behaviors that are not productive, effective and efficient often lead to the organism's death. So, the answer to the question what is the Perfect Government is, depends who you are asking. One of the greatest deceptions our government has perpetrated is this meme of there is ONE society which is best for ALL people. Common sense will tell you that is simply not true. It is almost like the term Social Justice.

Chapter 31
Leftist, Collectivist, Globalists Arguments

As a final thought, I would like to include some conversations I've had with leftists and the arguments they put up against this book. I was part of the brainwashing Marxist public school system in America and then when into the Leftist University system of America where Democrats outnumber Republicans 40-1 and Socialists outnumber Democrats. I had to endure the most illogical, falsehoods and lies for many years. While the elite, protected, privileged, rich, cloistered, anointed ones spoke about the poor unwashed masses and how the elite, protected, privileged, rich, cloistered, anointed ones were mistreating them.

1. Not every act is selfish.

Yes, it is. That's all I can say. Every person is selfish and every act they commit is 100% selfish. Collectivists say not every act a person does is in their own self-interest. I am always able to make the argument of whether its mother Theresa or their own mother every act they have ever witnessed is selfish. If you look if you look at the basic matrix of gaming theory everyone in every act is maximizing their pleasure and minimizing their pain. Mother Teresa can be shown with her stance on birth control and the huge amount of money and publicity that she raised for the Catholic Church a great deal of which never went to help the poor was a very self-serving woman just like every human being. She benefited greatly from her actions and the Catholic Church benefited greatly from her actions. Both were in a mutually profitable relationship. Leftists will always try to come up with a single solitary example of someone who at one time did not benefit from an interaction. Most of these are a simple miscalculation by the person. A female who puts up with a male's crap thinking she will get a ring or he makes more money than he really said he did. Or a male who puts up with the female's crap thinking he will get sex or that she is nicer then she really is. Perhaps with her makeup, perfume, diet and working out, push-up bra, and hair extensions, she had sold herself as being far more attractive than she really was.

There are other examples when people are fooled and have done acts that did not benefit them but in most cases, they end up regretting them dramatically. Men who go through a midlife crisis realizing they have struggled and worked in raised children and sacrificed thinking it would lead to a

220

carrot at the end when the carrot was never there were still acting selfish the whole time. Women after raising kids, and sacrificing for a family after 20 years looking up and saying is this all there is, just miscalculated they were being selfish the whole time. The fact that they were fooled or brainwashed or just did not think out the full extent of the contract and question their options, maybe these women didn't think they had any other choice so they were making the most selfish decision based on limited information. Some women of low self-esteem who don't know their true worth might sell themselves cheaper than they would have if they had known better.

I heard a statistic that well over half of older people if they had to do it all over again would decide not to have children. So, if they knew it was such a sacrifice they would not have done it. They admit they are not self-sacrificing they just made the wrong decision. Many people having children and sacrificing for children was not really even a choice. Liberals always try to come up with some example to support their communist utopia that people are not selfish and we all want to work for others good. But if you examine their actions closely and weigh the costs and benefits with objective open-minded assessment it can be shown that they did behave in a way that profited them the most.

Of course, there are mentally ill people whose brains do not function right, who have an organic problem, a trauma in childhood, a brain injury perhaps a severely limited IQ however these people are not the exception to the rule. They are the exception which proves the rule. They are damaged people they are no more helpful in understanding the general way people work than looking at a wrecked car in a junkyard with its engine ripped out and saying see not every car has an engine. That does not explain how a car is supposed to run. It is usually not worth the time but even if you look at those unusual cases the childhood abuse or whatever, those people are doing something to get some type of pleasure out of it. There is some profit driven motive in their action. Even if a normal person would not see profit in their action. A woman who was sexually abused as a little girl might pursue a very destructive lifestyle and relationship with future men but if you could look clearly into her mind she is still doing what profits her the most perhaps a real connection in a meaningful way with a man would be far too painful so she pursues a very promiscuous lifestyle or perhaps she wishes to take control of her sexuality and show she can turn it on or off at her command, finally she gets to say yes or no. And the pleasure of doing this even though it might cause her overall a very destructive and painful lifestyle is what she is pursuing if only for a short term. Perhaps the girl who is a fat girl now can get some pleasure by controlling what goes in or out of her mouth and the pain of anorexia is offset by the pleasure of finally being able to take charge of this former food addiction.

The individual cases of strange behavior which make the world seem very messed up is probably equal the number of people in the world and to understand every single one of them would take an inordinate amount of time. However, when you look closely enough you will see that every action a person does is selfish. It does not matter in the long run if every single inner interaction or activity is 100% understood. I teach Physics and explain clearly to the students we don't really understand what gravity is, they can't tell you if a graviton is exchange particle or a wave. They cannot tell you why the gravitational constant is what it is, but they can tell from observation that gravity works. We can land a man on the moon without understanding every instance of what gravity is how it works and what it is doing. The same can be said for arguing against the selfish nature of individuals. I can make as many arguments against gravity as I could against the selfish acts observed nature but it still does not change the fact that the theory of gravity explains exactly what we observe the universe doing and the theory of selfish acts explains exactly what we see individuals, organizations societies and governments doing. I also teach zoology and ecology and for 30 years have said to my students if you can show me a single act in nature that is truly altruistic and not selfish i.e. does not benefit the organism or its genes then I will give you an A in the course. I have never had a student claimed there A yet. I should not have to give out the A because common sense will tell you any organism that puts itself or its genes at a disadvantage to other organisms will go extinct and not exist to be the representative example. And this is exactly what we see in nature. From termites to wasps to lions to coral reefs to dolphins to prairie dogs to crows to baboons we see that all of them have maintained stable organizations with each individual acting 100% selfish.

2. Not everyone is motivated by selfishness.

Leftists and globalists, nonprofit charity ownership, etc. will tell you that good people are motivated to help others. Every beauty pageant contestant will tell you all they want, is world peace. Of course, this is not true. One of the easiest ways to make money in America is to start a nonprofit organization they even have majors in colleges offering good pay called nonprofit organizational management. People going to college are seeking these majors because they pay more than a business degree. And of course, the beauty contestants want to win the beauty contest far more than they want world peace. They are simply saying what will win the contest for them that is profit them the most. They are saying the most selfish, self-serving answer to the question they possibly can. If there is another way to answer the question and win the contest they would answer that way. I'm sure if they had beauty contests in fundamentalist Muslim countries the contestants would say "All I want to do is kill the infidels." Which is exactly the same answer as a beauty contest in the politically correct West saying, "All I want is world peace." They would do it.

Again there are people who have been trained, indoctrinated, and brainwashed into feeling pleasure when those acts are done and are conditioned to feel pain when not acting in the government approved way. But that is just proof that brainwashing, reeducation, indoctrination, works if it is used effectively not that people aren't motivated by selfishness. For brain washing to work it must also use the principles of gaming theory and selfishness. We simply must make the improper action so painful that the persons selfish desire to avoid pain and seek pleasure makes them behave in the way we want. It in no way refutes the fact that everyone is selfish, it proves that fact. This is not much different than a parasite which can go into the brain of an ant and alter their behavior to no longer work for the colony but to act in the best interest of the parasite. This is obviously an infection, a sickness, a parasite, a trick used to bypass the brains natural programing.

Another argument I frequently get over the years from my friends who are cops, or military is we are doing our jobs to save lives. We do our jobs to help people, not to make money. I always say that is poppycock and if offered the imaginary choice. A genie comes up and says I will give you a job that pays twice as much and is twice as easy but helps no one you wouldn't take it? I will sometimes be told by cops and military, no I wouldn't? I don't believe this answer and explain you could get twice the money, give your children so much more and never risk your life again or work hard and get a better retirement? You wouldn't take that you must be so selfish and not love your wife and kids? It is surprising how many cops and military stick to their answer. An interesting side note is two other groups teachers and firemen who also help society a great deal will almost always answer the question double the pay, halve the work twice the retirement. Heck yes sign me up. I don't know what this means and my sample size is too small to be conclusive but it's interesting.

3. I am my brother's keeper (master)

This is a constant reason given by the leftists, collectivists. That they want to help everyone and they are trying to save people from themselves. I heard an honest girl once say she went on a missionary trip and all they did was go to one poor village after another sightseeing and taking pictures, of the poor like animals at a zoo. All these rich kids simply using it as a photo stop and that no poor person was helped in this. No one has a right to decide for someone else what is good for them. You decide that I should exercise every day are you going to pass a law that says I must walk 3 miles a day. Are you going to pass a law that says I cannot eat Twinkies because I don't know what's good for me? Alcohol is not good we should outlaw that. It has been tried but maybe it wasn't tried right we could do prohibition right this time. Even though the record shows it caused far more harm than it caused good. (but I'm sure they meant well)

To be objective I am not sure its arrogance that causes certain liberals to assume they should be their brother's keeper because that is just a nice, or camouflaged way to say my brothers master. So maybe they are not arrogant but down right evil. Wanting to control others. Having listened to the intolerant left many times I am sure it's not kindness its ranchor with a drive to dominate and control and subjugate that motivates them just as much as good intent.

The collectivists argument that we all are our brother's keeper and that it takes a whole village to raise a child and everyone needs to be in everyone else's business and people are really too stupid to know what's good for them so the state should decide what's good for them is such a dangerous way of thinking and a slippery slope that has no logical stopping point. The logical conclusion being that we all live like an ant colony or termite mound or beehive. It is the classic argument that the individual's subservience to society. When the individual feels, society reels. Perhaps with collective hive mind and the proper pushes from agencies we can get everyone's mind preaching the party line. Which is the opposite of Nietzsche's philosophy that all of society should be set up to create the Ubermenschen

4. Government is needed to protect us from corporations.

This is another area where the logic of leftists, collectivists, and pro big government people escapes me. They start with the reasonable premise which I do agree with.

A group of people organized and having more power than another group of people will take advantage of the weaker group of people. This has been shown to happen repeatedly. This goes back into prehistory and has been going on for millions of years that way. Larger stronger groups of people have always taken advantage of smaller weaker groups of people. And when I start discussions with leftists I have this common ground with them. But then their solution to this problem is to create a government, an organized group of people so big and strong that group of people can stand up to them. It was this reason and for this reason alone that the 2nd amendment was created.

The idea is that this huge, strong, powerful, organization the government will protect the smallest, tiniest, weakest, organization the common people. From the medium strength organization, the corporations. As if it is not plainly obvious that the super strong government, and the medium strong corporations will just work together to victimize the super weak common people. This is a lapse of logic that I find difficult to fathom. It is like saying the sheep need a very large and powerful tiger to protect them from the jackals. Anyone with a brain will see that the tigers will kill the sheep and let the jackals pick the bones. Only the millionaire sheep in protected pens and gated communities are safe in that kind of environment.

One excuse the liberal sheep make I have heard because I have listened to these people is that the government is there to help the people and the corporations are only there to make a profit. Really? The tiger is there to protect the sheep and the evil jackals would eat the sheep if the tiger wasn't there protecting them. People who go into government don't want money and power? Really? Only good altruist guys are attracted to government? This is so illogical and far from the reality. When it is obvious that the most power-hungry people are attracted to government.

It also stuns me in how stupid people are. They know for a fact that the person running in the Other political party is an evil power-hungry, profit driven individual but the person running for office in their political party is a nice, altruistic, nonpower seeking individual who only wants to help. It is as if the government is not like any other organism which wants to grow, increase in size, consume more resource and make profit. Why would the government want to consume corporations when it's so much easier to consume citizens? And when the elite in the government and the elite in the corporations make up less than 1% of the population why wouldn't they work together to victimize the other 99% of the population who are such easy targets?

There is another argument that the government is answerable to the citizens. Leftists basically say that citizens control the government and not the other way around. They say that citizens vote in the government and so they have a huge say in what kind of government governs them. But they don't have any say in corporations who are only out for themselves. But the government is out to help the people. Even when I point out that the government has done

229

everything in its power to make itself NOT answerable to the citizens for example they have gerrymandered districts where it is almost impossible for the candidate not chosen by the Republican or the Democratic Party to be reelected. In 80% of the states because of the way electoral votes are counted. It doesn't matter how you vote your votes are guaranteed to either the Republican or the Democrat candidate. And even if you are in a swing state your vote still doesn't count unless it comes down to you as being the single deciding vote. Which never has happened. Not only that but being 1/300,000,000 voters does not give you much say in anything. Imagine if you owned 000,000,003 % of a company well actually that would be much better as you actually would own something.

Leftists don't seem to understand that according to their way of thinking people can make the government snap around and change to their will. However, when I point out things that the government does against the people for example the German government is flooding its country with refugees that most of the German people don't want. The leftists will immediately say but that is for the common good. Or they will say yes governments should be progressive in their thinking and sometimes do things that are unpopular. What this simply means is they want the government to do what they want but not the will of most people. This proves my earlier point that governments don't have to do the will of the people anyway. As far as having influence over an organization or an entity American citizen have much more influence over a corporation than they do a government. When Chick-fil-A made an unpopular decision and the citizens boycotted them their profits went down. It would only take a week of boycotting

Starbucks to severely hurt that company.   If the US government did something unpopular nothing would happen to them in a week, a month or a year or ever. If McDonald's made a grossly negative statement the American citizens could boycott that restaurant and destroy it in a month. There is nothing the government has to fear from its citizens there is no such thing as a boycott. There is no way American citizens can withhold their taxes from the American government. If Ford Motor Company upset the American public with some egregious act every citizen that did not buy a Ford car would cost the company $30,000 immediately within 6 months Ford would have to answer to this or die. But the American government has nothing to fear like this.

It is a lie that Americans get to pick a new president every 4 years. The American citizen only gets a choice between 2 people not anyone. And those 2 people have passed the test and become anointed by the political machine. The lesser of 2 evils, is all the American people get to cast between. Imagine if there were only 2 jobs to do Brick layer or Drywaller and you got to pick between those 2 most people would realize the system was rigged. But somehow when the same choices given among presidential candidates everyone thinks the system is fair.

The fallacy that the Leftists make that government is answerable to the people but corporations are not answerable to the people, is a fantasy. It is a lapse of logic and an example of the shallowest most incomplete thinking. Or it is a downright lie and they know better. I tend to get angry and think they are just lying and no one can be that stupid as they claim.

Collectivists want a government big enough and strong enough to give you everything not realizing that it is now big enough and strong enough to take everything from you. And it is so big and strong that it no longer has anything to fear from you. And it can cooperate with its much smaller partners the corporations to really take advantage of the tiny weak individual. I understand the rich Champaign socialists and the rich powerful limousine liberals who laugh all the way to the bank. Living in the barn while the tiger prowls outside occasionally eating an outside sheep. Smiling saying we need the tiger big and strong to protect us from the Jackals. But I don't understand the vulnerable outside sheep siding with the in the barn sheep saying we need this big tiger to protect up from the jackals.

5. Socialism could work If everyone would just play nice.

This is the mantra of Marxists if we would just have everyone do socialism right it would work. If everyone would just be nice we could all have a great life. If everyone would just cooperate and if everyone would act in the best interest of all then everything would be wonderful. Communism really works we just need to give it one more try. To this I answer of course you're right if gravity didn't exist I wouldn't fall down. If I could breathe underwater I wouldn't drown and if my aunt had balls she would be my Uncle. (although I guess this is politically incorrect now)

This mantra ignores all reality and the collectivists the socialists know it. But their only solution to this is to fight human nature so fiercely and have a government so huge, so powerful, so rich, so intrusive, with so many guards that it forces everyone to act against their nature. Not realizing that the cost of watching everybody all the time, deincentivizing all initiative and hard work and not rewarding creativity, innovation and extra effort costs far more than having a freer society where people work hard get rewarded for it and are able to exercise their free will.

The answer to this question is basically people are not going to play fair and if you have enough guards to force them to play fair you make the world more unfair. You make it more unfair that it would be if you had just left it alone. Nothing is more ironic and unfair than trying to force unequal people to be equal

6. But the Intentions are Good.

This is one of the most frustrating answers leftists give. I cannot comprehend how this argument is even made because I have heard it from many individuals over many years in many places. So, it must be part of the Marxist playbook. If I had only heard it once I would have attributed it to that single person was absolutely crazy, mentally unhinged, or with an organic brain problem. However, this excuse is used as if it is a good point. I can say communism takes over and kills hundreds of millions of people and never works. Look

1917 Communists take Russia....1920s famine in Russia.

1949 Communists take China....1950s famine in China.

1978 Communists take Ethiopia....1980s famine in Ethiopia.

And the people will look at me and answer
"But the intentions were good" or
"They meant well"
As if that wipes the whole slate clean and brings back millions of horribly killed people?

Again, I cannot comprehend this stance that is so common among the left. It's like a get out of jail free card that absolved all responsibility and washes away all sin. In this regard, the leftist, socialist, hippie is just like the fundamentalist Christian who argues that the most horrible serial killer and violent human being on earth could just say "I believe in Jesus" before being killed in the electric chair and live for eternity in paradise.

In an argument with the globalist collectivist leftist a pro big government liberal if you point out every example of communism, socialism and big government harming people it is overwhelming and undeniable. If you say look at North Korea and look at South Korea. If you say compare East Germany with West Germany during the Cold War one communist, one capitalist. If you compare communist China with nationalist Taiwan. And say to them clearly which place would you rather have lived which place would you want to raise your children in? If you explain all the harm and murders and death and pain caused by huge, powerful, communist, socialist, government. If you explain the beginning of the United States of America when communism was tried and failed. How the original colonies tried communism and nearly starved to death and it was only when people were given their own land farm that production picked up enough to feed everyone. If you show all the examples of all the communes started as social experiments in America with a 100% failure rate. If you explain the high standard of living that free enterprise has given the world and citizens in those countries compared to government controlled countries. The leftists will eventually when faced with this mountain of evidence fall back to the excuse. "But they meant well." It had good intentions. "They wanted it to work". It is as if murder and torture misery pain and a low standard of living were just accidental outcomes of big government collectivism and should be given a free pass because that isn't what they meant.

As a young kid, I pointed out to an adult how our school had been destroyed by Social Justice how destroyed the schools harming all the children. And this adult said. "But the intentions were good" as if that fixed everything. I don't know what argument can be used against this state of mind because it seems to be universal among the liberal collectivists. The big government meant well and even if it's outcomes are different than its intentions it's the intentions that count not the outcomes.

7. The Government is not Force.

The leftist, communist, big powerful government fanboy has a duplicity of logic when it comes to force. If force is used by a man protecting his home, family, car, property, from an aggressor or intruder it is a horrible. No human has a right to take another person's life. No one gets to decide if any person lives or dies.

But if the Government does it that's fine. In fact, it isn't even force. Every stand your ground law, every idea that a father or husband can shoot a burglar invading his home or property is considered unnecessary violence, a bad use of force by the person endorsing big government. They idealize a utopia of everyone living together in peace and harmony and with no one disagreeing with the huge centralized government that takes money from certain people and gives it to other people against the will of the people. This government makes polices that hurt some groups and helps other groups. This giant unstoppable government gives the stick to some behaviors and the carrot to other behaviors. However, the Liberal will never admit that the government is simply force.

As George Washington said government is force, only force, and nothing but force. I have even heard these slave minded r-selected people explain that taxation is voluntary. They will claim that people pay taxes voluntary? When I say No you illogical person that is why taxes are collected with a threat. if you don't pay your taxes the government will kill and torture you. I got oh no. The government doesn't kill anyone. I say don't pay your taxes and you go to jail. If you resist going to jail they will defeat your resistance if its weak and if your resistance is strong they will kill you. And if you are just shot up or subdued you will then go to jail to be tortured. The collectivist will smile and say. Oh no look see this famous rich guy who owes on his taxes he is not being killed. To which I say. No rich people hire lawyers who can go to court and get appeals and continuances not average poor people. The IRS will impose fines to collect more than it is owed. So, it is profitable for the IRS to behave this way. The simple fact of the matter is. Submitting to the biggest, strongest, bully the government does not mean you voluntarily submitted to them. Giving them all the power and pretending they are not using that power to extract taxes and control behavior is preposterous.

I wonder if a psychologist could look at this form of slave minded, Stockholm syndrome effect going on inside the pro big government people's head. As I consider what is happening it is simply this. The big government fanboy likes big government and so if big government bullies and takes things and behaves exactly as the leftist wants. The leftist does not recognize this as violence, force or threat. It is much like a weakling who does not have the ability or courage to take your wallet but will gladly watch and enjoy a stronger person to take your wallet. This is especially true if the stronger mugger gives him a few dollars to go along with him. Perhaps the stronger mugger will even let the liberal pick the shoes off the knocked-out victim.

The argument that government is not violent force used by people who want bigger government is a supreme act of deception and camouflage. Of course, people doing threats and violence for their cause is not acknowledges as bullying by the intolerant left. To acknowledge this truth would be as unprofitable for them as a leopard hiding in a leafy background to give up his camouflage of spots. Why would they pull off their mask of tolerance and show an intolerant face? I hear people say government will not kill you, they will fine you or put you in jail. What if you don't pay the fine. Well then you are thrown in jail. What if you don't accept going to jail. Well then, they will capture you and put force you in jail. Well what if you resist capture then they will kill you. So, if you don't comply with the government it will kill you. This is very simple and true of every government. But if a person cannot accept this as a fact means they are not discussing anything in good faith. Government is force and will kill you if you don't comply or resist.

8. The most successful societies today are partially socialist.

Leftists love to point out that some of the richest, most prosperous, countries with the highest standard of living are socialist or at least partially socialist. Like all people selfishly trying to win for their side and not trying to find the truth they ignore almost all the data. They almost always choose a country which has some unfair advantage or is on the road to extinction or only paint have the picture. For example, they will choose Norway which has more oil than people it is so rich from the North Sea oil fields and has such a tiny population. 3 million people and their defense is paid for by the United States. A well-educated, fully homogeneous population that still has cohesive tribal values rooted in a long-established past that has always discouraged cheating. That society can afford to give away a lot of social programs to its relatively small closely related tribe of individuals. The liberals love to compare a technologically advanced country with some elements of socialism to a technologically backward country without elements of socialism.

I once heard the president of a nonprofit organization who is working on homelessness in Hawaii was trying to get the government of Hawaii to give vouchers to low income people so that would use them to pay part of the rent. Of course, he wanted his nonprofit organization to gather up the people and hand the vouchers out to them all the while taking his cut he was one of the most profit motivated individuals I had ever met. I listened to him give a speech to a group of citizens and he explained how Singapore handled its homeless population so well. He went on how many countries handle their homeless problem so much better the United States. I sat in the audience and having been to Singapore and having a Singapore roommate in college knew being homeless in Singapore was a crime. That's how they handle their homeless problem. Even in the days of Google we don't have many people able to think or look up things when given statements they should question.

Liberals seem to confuse causation with correlation it's not that these countries become socialist and then get rich, prosperous, and everyone has a high standard of living. It's the other way around it's that the countries that become rich have so much extra money that they can afford to now be generous it doesn't cost them as much to give away money. Big government doesn't cause wealth. Wealth causes big government.

Statetheists those who worship the state love to compare two very different counties and pretend they are the same. A society with many advantages over another with few. It is beyond apples and oranges and then pretend that the only difference between the 2 is one is socialist and the other is not. Norway doesn't even have to pay for its own defense that bill is carried by the United States. Norway is isolated by huge ocean and is not easily invaded. It has many advantages but I still would suggest it is not going to be a stable country. Norway's neighbor Sweden will probably not exist in another 50 years because of its social policies. It is an example of a once successful society that is on the decline and on its way to death. To point out these socialist countries as examples of vigor and health makes as much sense as pointing out the professional athlete on a cocaine binge and saying see cocaine is good for you. He will not last long doing those behaviors. Those were not the behaviors that make him successful. It was his success that allowed him enough money to buy the cocaine.

In the animal kingdom, we see examples of such organizations that have survived millions of years. Leftists like to use examples of rich, decadent, spoiled societies with no competition that have only survived for 100 years as a stable success story. This is simply not seeing the whole picture and seeing in the long-term. So, to answer this question, no the richest societies were not created by ignoring reality and discarding facts which big government advocates, the Statetheists must do. Socialism and communism do not create wealth. Great wealth allows socialism to form. No society started out with socialism. It is only after wealth and success is established that socialism can creep in.